KIPAWA:
Portrait
of a People

Kermot A. Moore

> They want to take our land:
> Are those people crazy?
> *An Elder of Kipawa*

HIGHWAY BOOK SHOP
COBALT, ONTARIO P0J 1C0

© Copyright 1982 by Kermot A. Moore, copyright renewed 1986 by Theresa Moore and Gwendolyn Moore

All rights reserved. No part of this book may be used or reproduced in any manner whatever without written permission except in the case of brief quotations embodied in critical articles and reviews.

ISBN 0-88954-243-0

Published by Highway Book Shop, Cobalt, Ontario, Canada P0J 1C0

Acknowledgement

Thanks are due Canada Council for its support of the research and writing of this book and to Mr. Craig Fraser for his donation toward its production. I would also like to thank the many Natives of Kipawa and elsewhere, without whose information and encouragement this work would not have seen print. Nevertheless, responsibility for the facts presented here and their interpretation is mine alone.

—K.M.

Heritage

Something has been lost,
or if not lost, buried
    like the paths of the trapper
under sidewalk cement, under
harsh apartment buildings, under
diseased dark lines
    of writers telling it
  like it is.

We should go home again
where the highway ripples
  out of the north
    flowing
thru lonely landscapes
the old painters and poets knew.

Should seek the river's source
where turning gravel road
trickles away
  from the main route,

where the going's harder
and has to be traversed
by heart,
    in moccasins
perhaps,
    thru underbrush
that blinds the literal eye
and tangles the logical
foot.

Something remains:
something green as
  sweetgrass after rain

and growing.

                Dorothy Farmiloe

To my Grandmother Wabi-ko-kok-oho

Daughter of Chief Wabiko

Contents
Page

1	CHAPTER ONE	The Awakening
4	CHAPTER TWO	The Early Days
12	CHAPTER THREE	Foreign Disease
33	CHAPTER FOUR	Land Use and Ownership
43	CHAPTER FIVE	Spiritual Beliefs
51	CHAPTER SIX	The Fur Trade
70	CHAPTER SEVEN	Agriculture and its Social Effects
93	CHAPTER EIGHT	Lumbering
117	CHAPTER NINE	Forest Fire Protection
121	CHAPTER TEN	Tourism
133	CHAPTER ELEVEN	The Move from the Communities
142	CHAPTER TWELVE	Hunting and Fishing Rights versus Zone d'Amenagement et de Conservation

Page

146	CHAPTER THIRTEEN The Trapline System
155	CHAPTER FOURTEEN Municipal Government
161	CHAPTER FIFTEEN Land of the Nishnabi—Today and Tomorrow

Introduction

My purpose for writing this book is to give the Native people of Kipawa a record of their past, to rekindle for the elders the glorious memories of a time when a knowledge of nature and the skills of survival were the highest attributes of manhood and womanhood; to reach my middle-aged confreres, who seem to have forgotten who they are . . . Perhaps the pride of other years will find a place of nourishment in their hearts and minds. And for the children—if by these writings they can gain an understanding of their origins, new hope may yet spring. If the children can gain some insight into their past, their illustrious, hard-working ancestors, they may find the courage to attack the inequities of today's situation with the stubbornness and stoic determination of their forefathers.

To this end, I am reviewing the past from every source of indigenous recollection, legends and customs which have almost been forgotten in our time, and attempting to reassess the tragedies that befell our people from contact with the Europeans. A knowledge of the past, as every student of history is aware, is essential for solving problems of the present.

The principal source of this history is the oral accounts of the elders. Evident in those memories is the *strong spirit of survival* that carried our ancestors through countless years of tragedy. If the pathetic despair can be erased from the present generation of Kipawa's Native people, by revealing a prouder history of better days, then, perhaps they will find the courage to be their own masters. The present situation threatens a once-proud people with oblivion or annihilation because of their own lack of vision and willingness to stand up for their rights on the one hand, and the preponderance of colonial bureaucratic officialdom on the other.

In writing this history I am writing for a people who do not have a tradition of reading; in fact, many of our elders do not read at all. Therefore, reading and explanation for some elders will be necessary. Where possible pictures will be used to illustrate a way of life that was rigorous, yet satisfying to the body and spirit.

This will be the first history written from a Native point of view, by a Native person of the Kipawa territory. History by its very nature is biased. Although events may be factual, histories rarely are; everything written about events carries the personal bias of the writer. Since the history of Canada is, so far, the perception of a colonial mentality, it is subject to the bias and distortion of that mentality. Regarding the principles of history writing, Cervantes, author of *Don Quixote*, once wrote, "History is a Sacred kind of writing, because truth is essential to it." These are very high principles, very difficult to follow when you take up a position on the other side of the looking glass. To explain that remark I must say that a Native person reading Canadian history comes away with a distinct impression that colonial historians stood before a looking glass and saw only themselves. Now the time has come to look from the other side.

In researching records of the fur companies, the missionaries, and the explorers, you soon see that most of the "Indians" mentioned are those who helped a foreign cause or mission. Europeans judged the Native people as good or bad "Indians," depending on whether they supported or hindered European causes or missions. Until recently, our school books reflected that attitude. In time other criteria were established, that demanded European ways and values, as well as European custom and religion. Our history books still reflect that attitude. This history will be free of that bias.

Similarly, the field of anthropology shows this bias by attempting to prove that the indigenous people of the Americas came from Asia over an ice and land bridge. It is as if to say that our indigenous ancestors could walk only in one direction—west to east. Whether man walked across an ice bridge ten thousand years ago or over a land bridge thirty thousand years earlier is unimportant. All such theories are speculation confirmed to a greater or lesser degree by evidence that is often mutually conflicting.

We know that the species called "man" has spread throughout the globe and scientists claim evidence of human habitation in the Americas forty thousand years ago. Therefore it is important for the Native people to realize that their ancestors explored and inhabited every region of this vast hemisphere thousands of years before recorded history. Great civilizations came and went during those times. Perhaps the romance of those eons of time in the hemisphere has embedded in the Native psyche the deep and abiding love and respect which most Natives feel for the land. In that regard the indigenous American's attachment to the land is no different from the European's love for Europe, the Asian's feeling toward Asia, or the African's claim to Africa. The very essence of our being is this attachment, a love immeasurable by dollars.

The elders whom I interviewed greatly enjoyed recalling their youth and sharing their memories. In some instances they could recall events of the six or seven previous generations. In order to establish a time frame, however, I read archival material of fur companies, missionaries, lumber companies, and anthropologists, as well as books by reputable authors on those subjects.

Since "history is people," this book will recreate the past with stories and anecdotes of the people of those times; not all the people, or all the stories, but, I hope enough to give a flavor of their way of life. How were family hunting territories established? How did a man conserve his animals to ensure the survival of his family and the preservation of land for his children and his children's children? How did the original people view land ownership? What cultural and spiritual traditions did our ancestors develop and how did those traditions respond to the pressures of economic and social change?

While reconstructing a genealogy of the people of Kipawa, I borrowed old photographs, some of which are used to reconstruct the characters of people and things that made our history. I know that those elders, unable to read, will relive old times by seeing these pictures and by having these stories read to them by those who can. In turn, if the elders can add to the stories and events covered here, they will help the young appreciate this heritage they share.

I use the word Métis to describe people of mixed European and Native blood. Since 1967, Métis has become synonymous with the word half-breed and accepted nationally by people of that lineage. Since half-breed was commonly used in the Kipawa territory in times past, however, I will use it wherever it is historically correct to do so.

I use the word "Indian" in this book on occasion when speaking of the indigenous inhabitants of the Americas. "Indian" as used in this country is a label—not a nationality. Obviously, the real Indians are the 700 million inhabitants of India, with strong identities, cultures and histories associated with that nation. Since the name is colonial convention of this country, however, there are certain situations, such as reference to the "Indian Act," or the regulations that flow from that Act, when the use is unavoidable.

For the same reason Algonquin and Ojibway are also meaningless terms. We are Nishnabi. If by convention Algonquin or Ojibway must appear in this book the reader should take it to mean Nishnabi.

To the Native people of Kipawa I say: we must explore our Nishnabi roots, for we are ancient dwellers in an ancient land. We are as indigenous as the soil that nourished our roots. The pride of *being* is essential in the forward march of any people. People must have the pride and courage to decide what they want for themselves and their children. Under the colonial system we have rejected ourselves and our past. It is high time to question the values of that system. The wrongs are obvious. We must reverse those teachings if we are to make a new start.

For now at least, we have fallen into the double traps of alcoholism and apathy. There are many reasons for this: for one, rejection figures strongly—rejection of ourselves and the rejection of our ancestry. When we reject ourselves, we lose pride in ourselves. We must know our past and the present if we are to live well in the future. Our pride, our dignity, and our personal worth must be born again. Self-esteem and positive goals in life are essential ingredients to our own betterment as a people.

Only when the Native people of Kipawa themselves decide to change those conditions will their bleak situation improve. If this book sparks revolutionary thinking among our people, then my heart will gladden, for real progress can only come through the people's awakening and their determination to improve themselves. To help my people to be themselves and to be proud of the fact, I have written this book.

CHAPTER ONE

The Awakening

"Are you here for the meeting tonight?"

My sister, Theresa, stood at the doorway as I walked up to my parents' home in Kipawa. I had just arrived from North Bay.

"No," I answered. "What meeting?"

Hesitating for a moment, she started to describe the events of the past week.

"Everyone along the lakeshore has gotten a letter from Jolette." Rejean Jolette is the public notary for the district that includes Kipawa. "He represents Gordon Creek Improvement Company in this matter and he has told everyone to cough up ten thousand dollars to pay for their lots."

"*What*! Where in Hell does he get this idea?"

"Here." She handed me the letter. "See for yourself."

I read through it. My first reaction was that the letter was a con job. To begin with, it was in mimeographed form.

"Everyone's received the letter—even people who have died or moved away," my sister added. "Everyone's stuck with the bill; even people with small lots."

Furthermore, it was in French. Since Jolette has dealt with the people of this community as a public official for the past twenty years, he knew that all our schooling is in English and that few of us are fluent in French. So he obviously didn't want many people to understand the contents of that letter.

Besides, he wasn't about to reveal the company he was actually representing. The Gordon Creek Improvement Company had been a subsidiary of several logging firms organized at the turn of the century to improve the shoreline for driving logs from Kipawa Lake to the Ottawa River. But the log drives had ceased twenty years ago. So, Jolette's affiliation with the Gordon Creek Improvement Company meant nothing.

"O.K., so what time's the meeting being held, and where?" I asked, after reading through the letter several times.

"Eight o'clock, at the basement of the church," she replied, glancing at her watch. "We'll barely make it on time."

I had returned to Kipawa to gather the rest of the information

1

needed to complete this book. I couldn't have come at a better time. Here was the start of another land-grab, and I had landed right in the middle of it. So, I didn't mind going to an unexpected meeting.

It was edging toward darkness and starting to rain as we drove up to the parking lot in back of the church. We could see that the place was packed. The lot was full, and when we entered the church, we saw a crowd standing at the doorway to the basement.

I chatted with some of the people. Some had never attended a public meeting before. To get them out here took a land-grabbing proposition like this. Here was a common enemy, an enemy clothed in legal jargon, backed by the gun of the police and the army. Never before had the people been so united. It took the threat of loss of their homes to shake them from their apathy.

As the chairman called the meeting to order, I sensed a determination mixed with apprehension. Some of the people suggested to me that bullets would fly if this land-grab—some called it extortion—were allowed to proceed. There was no way these people would give up their homes. Even a few non-Native cottagers were here; they, too, had received their notices.

Also attending was the executive staff of the Laurentian Alliance of Métis and Non-Status Indians along with the Land Title Director and legal counsel.

The legal counsel began the meeting with a review of the land situation. Jolette's letter demanded one thousand dollars from each homeowner to open negotiations and an additional nine thousand dollars within twelve days. The client would have to produce his deed at his own expense—for some, this would mean a costly title search.

An open discussion followed the review. The legal counsel brought up a story of a similar case. "Ted Mongrain received a letter from a lawyer back in 1973," he reported. "He was told to pay up five thousand dollars or lose his property." Mongrain's home had been located on a tiny patch of land. He had fought the order and won. Although the Mongrain case was discussed point by point at the gathering, nothing was unearthed to reveal the identity of the speculators or the law that permitted them to expropriate the properties along the lakeshore.

As discussion proceeded, the mood of the people hardened. More questions arose. We had long known that these plots are the last vestige of the home and country of the Nishnabi (Algonquin) people. When would all this end? Should we bow to this piracy and become homeless in a land where our ancestors had trodden and paddled as free men since the beginning of time? Were we to allow ourselves to be cast adrift like the Boat People from Vietnam—refugees in our own land? Would we acquiesce in *death*? Or would we fight to reverse this attack?

In times past, we had not understood colonialism. We had trusted the government; we had worked hand in hand with the missionaries, the fur traders, the schools, the lumbermen, the mining surveyors, and even the mappers of our land. Now we saw that all our resources had gone—and were going still—to enrich the outsiders, and like the fangs of a hyena, the outsiders would turn those riches against us to threaten even the very homes we live in. For, even as we met, we did not know that a highway was planned to connect Manawaki to Ville-Marie, passing through Kipawa.

Perhaps we should not have been so naive. That was now past history—our survival as a people was at stake, and remains so to this day. Are we to fight, we asked, to reverse this legal theft, or do we go down in history as a people who deserved their extinction because they were too gutless to fight?

As the meeting drew to a close, the people decided to prepare a petition stating the position of the Native people of Kipawa concerning the proposed expropriation. The Premier of Quebec would be asked to impose an injunction on the proceedings initiated by the Gordon Creek Improvement Company and to open a thorough investigation into the matter. The vote for the petition was unanimous. Even the non-Native cottagers, who formed one-fourth of the assembly, voted for the petition and offered their solid support.

As the people filed out of the basement, they knew this petition was but the first step of a long series of battles in this war against the unnamed threat to our lands. In the months ahead, there would be briefs to submit to hearings and cases to argue with officials from the Government of Quebec.

For now, there was nothing to do but wait. . . .

CHAPTER TWO

Kipawa: Geography and Historical Setting

The territory of Kipawa is a region of rough forest land dotted with lakes connected by streams. The village of Kipawa itself is located about eight miles north of the town of Temiscaming, near the boundary separating northwestern Quebec from northeastern Ontario (Map 2.1). The village of Kipawa is located on the southern shore of Lake Kipawa, which forms part of the drainage system that includes Lake Temiskaming and eventually empties into the Ottawa River. Lumbering, agriculture, and mining represent the mainstays of the territory, supplemented by seasonal tourism and occasional trapping. The territory was affirmed as Indian land through a proclamation made by King George III in 1763 and, for the Native residents of the area, this proclamation remains the foundation of their legal rights to the land. The Government of Canada has never dealt with Native claims in the vicinity of Kipawa—indeed, has never made settlements of any kind—so mining companies, lumbering firms, and private individuals have set up their operations without the Natives having relinquished or surrendered their rights. The Government of Quebec has never made treaties of any kind, required by the 1763 proclamation. This forms the basis of the conflict today, as shown in the preceding chapter.

The community is made up of some 230 Métis and 200 registered Indians together with several non-Native families. At one time, the entire territory was made up of hunters and gatherers who migrated seasonally from wintering to summering camps and back. Beaver, moose, deer, and other animals were the principal animals hunted and "farmed" to ensure a continuous supply. Bear was held sacred by the people, and so was hunted with respect.

Every family had its own territory (see Chapter Six and Map 6.1), knowing how much game was available each season, and so knowing how much could be taken without threatening its continuity. Anthropologists differ on whether the groups were bilateral extended families or full-blown clans, but there is a strong likelihood that they were organized into territories long before the Europeans came (see Chapter Six).

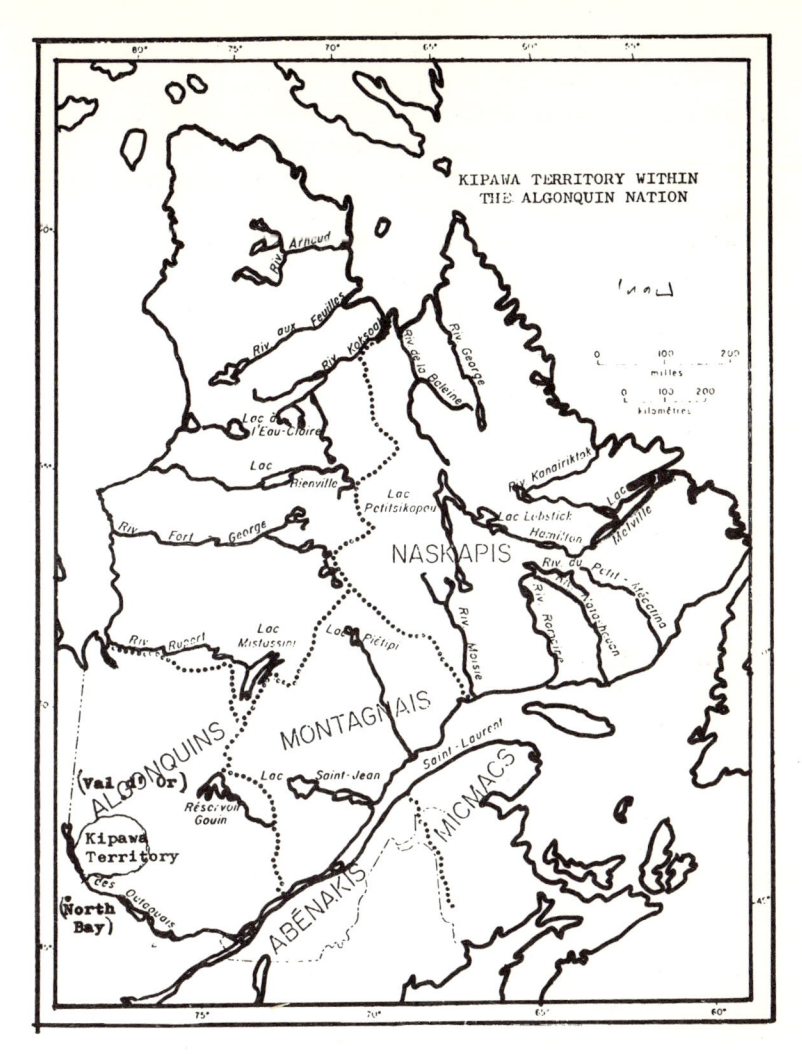

Map 2.1. The Territory of Kipawa.

With the coming of the Europeans and the fur trade, the Native population shifted their hunt to fur-bearing animals—beaver, marten, fisher, and others—while still relying on larger game for subsistence. Throughout the two hundred-year history of the fur trade, the Native people remained in the bush, going to villages only to sell their furs and obtain their supplies (Chapter Six). Only when the lumbering business required day-laborers and farmers to supply their horses with hay and their men with food did the Native people take up farming and living in villages. Even then, the Métis (mixed bloods) were the first to live in permanent settlements, to work for wages, and to farm (Chapter Seven). The principal village of the territory today is Kipawa.

While many Natives still hunt and trap, they have faced competition with non-Native poachers and trappers licensed by the government. The continuing erosion of Native land-rights, together with the steady depletion of plant and animal resources in the territory, have contributed to tensions that are now surfacing with meetings such as that described in the previous chapter.

What attitudes does the Native have toward all these developments? In this and succeeding chapters, I will show how the Native people have coped with the changes, sometimes how they have taken part in them as lumbermen, farmers and millworkers. Whatever his role might have been, however, the Native has never forgotten his land or his heritage. Perhaps the best start is the author's own history. We therefore begin with the memories of my grandmother, Wabi-ko-kok-oho.

***

Long time ago. Those were the words my grandmother used whenever she began to tell a story from the days of her childhood or the years before she was born. Today, that phrase conjures in my mind a clearing in the pine woods overlooking the lake, where an uncle of mine had recently built a cabin. The air smelled sweet and earthy from a freshly-hoed garden. The smoke of burning rotten wood curled through a loosely-stitched, cone-shaped moose hide, turning it slowly to golden brown. Tanning a moose hide was a back-breaking job, but the smoking—that was different. All my grandmother had to do was gather rotten wood and keep the smudge going. It was at times like this that she would sit back on a pile of balsam brush and tell us stories of her youth.

One day, when I was seven years old, I raced out of school to see what Grandma was doing. While she was sewing a moccasin, she told me a story that filled me with wonder—and a tinge of revulsion. Communication between us wasn't easy, for she spoke in pidgin English of a sort, and I spoke little Nishnabi.

"Long time ago," she started, "we paddle down to Mo-ne-ang."

Mo-ne-ang was her word for Montreal. She told how her father set out on his summer journey with his three canoes and three wives, joining two other families on the way. She spoke of it as if it were a sight-seeing vacation combined with a trip to sell their furs and buy provisions for the winter. I sat entranced as she described the rapids through which her father ran the canoes, the portages they made around the falls in the river, and the brisk winds they encountered on the big river. She recalled the lumber rafts of square timber and the farms that they saw as they paddled further down. As best she could, she described the fish they caught—"big black suckers," "snakefish," and others known to her only in the Native tongue. These fish were probably sturgeon and eel. Game must have been easy to hunt, for she explained how they would stop for a few days to smoke fresh meat and to pick berries.

Their destination was probably the trading post on the Lake of Two Mountains near Oka (Montreal). One might have expected to hear of hardships or ambushes on such a trip in those days, but, on the contrary, she spoke of the "Odawa" as a land of plenty.

Meeting other voyagers on the river usually meant joining them, for their destination and purpose were the same. These encounters gave them the chance to trade articles made in different regions by people speaking different dialects. Most of the people who joined their little convoy, it seems, spoke a Nishnabi tongue. Grandma mentioned how they shared the campgrounds with the Notoway (Mohawk) of Oka. Although the Nishnabi and Notoway were enemies at one time, she gave no hint of any hostility between them. If there had been fighting, Grandma would not have mentioned the fact in any event. She spoke as if adventure, beauty, and love had been gifts bestowed her from the Great Spirit, and that trust was with her till her final day.

I fidgeted a bit as the story came to an end, for my mind returned to the remark she had made about the three wives of her father. My indoctrination with the school and the Catholic Church had led me to believe that, though my own people were kind and good, "Indians" were evil. It wasn't that those institutions preached against our people. Rather, there was always some abstract "Indian" or "Indian" custom that existed somewhere else that was evil and had to be destroyed.

Not wanting to hear the worst about my great grandfather, it took me a while to work up enough courage to remind her, "Grandma, a man is not supposed to have three wives; that's what the priest says." She thought that one over for a while, for she had to translate Nishnabi customs to a language that gave her great difficulty.

Finally, she replied, "Long time ago, life very hard. Man work hard to get meat; sometime get killed; sometime disease from *Wumte-go-zi* [white man]. When man die, women, children have no one to get food. If brother die, brother who live take family. My father take two family—two brother die. Nene [I—that is, my grandmother] daughter of wife three. Each woman paddle [own] canoe."

There was an unexpected sequel to that story when I visited Bear Island, the centre of the Teme-agama, or the Nishnabi people of the Temagami region. I met Chief Gary Potts, and he began by showing me the genealogical charts of the Teme-agama Band.

It was like going back in history a hundred years. Those were mostly original names, haunting, yet when properly pronounced, had the echoes of the rivers, lakes, and forests. Others conjured images of birds and animals. He pointed at one chart, turned to me, and asked, "You come from Kipawa; have you ever heard of Juliette Wabiko?"

"No," I replied.

"Well," he said, "she married Ed Robinson at Wolf Lake."

Then the fact struck me. Juliette Wabiko was my own grandmother. When I was young, Grandma had told me that her name was Wabi-ko-kok-oho, which means "White Owl." I had not realized then that family names did not exist among the indigenous people before the arrival of the missionaries. Each person had an individual name; nothing more. Then as the missionaries baptized each individual, they recorded the father's individual name as the family's name. That was how my grandmother's father's name, Wabiko, became the family name after she left home. The English translation of Wabiko is "White Bear."

Examining the chart more closely, I remarked on a note beside my great grandfather's name, which read "two families."

"Something must be wrong there," I told Gary. "My grandmother spoke of three families."

"Well," replied Gary, "one of the women may have remarried.

Anyway, here's how the story goes around here. When the people here in Temagami first began to accept Christianity, Wabiko was chief, and he was having a hard time understanding the rules of this new teaching. Well, on one of his yearly summer visits, the missionary came up to Wabiko with a solemn expression on his face and told him to give up one of his wives, that it was against God's wishes for a man to have two wives. If he didn't abandon his evil ways, the priest went on, Wabiko would burn forever in the fires of Hell. The chief thought, at first, that it was a joke, because to him, it was crazy to think a woman could be left on her own to fend for her children. Still, the priest didn't give up his demand, so the chief left the gathering to think the matter over in the forest. He returned later with a terse solution: 'I shoot one wife—you paddle canoe.' "

There is no record of the priest's reply, but no one was shot. I have to think that Wabiko must have chuckled to himself over the whole affair. The clerical diary probably recorded that he remained a pagan.

This episode of Chief Wabiko and the priest points out the strength of the Native extended family. The Native cared for his brothers' families as much as he cared for his own. His relationship with his deceased brothers' wives was that of guardian, not that of husband. He merely followed a custom that the severity of life demanded at that time.

After visiting Chief Gary Potts in Temagami, I gradually pieced together the biography of my grandmother, Juliette Wabiko (Wabiko-kok-oho).

She was born in the territory of Temagami and as a young girl accompanied her family on canoe trips that saw most of the Ottawa River, North Temiskaming, and Kipawa territories. At sixteen, she married Edward Robinson, an Irish lumberman. Today, their descendants number more than 150. They settled at Wolf Lake, where they grew excellent crops. She was also good at raising foxes. One day, she caught two baby foxes and eventually bred twenty. Eventually, she gave up this venture when the price for fox pelts dropped, making it unprofitable.

After her husband died, she became even more active. She hoed fields by hand and grew vegetables for herself and others. She tanned hides, and made moccasins and snowshoes. In the spring of the year, she might even be seen in the bush with two of her

Juliette Wabiko (Wabi-ko-kok-oho).

granddaughters, for a couple of weeks, hunting beaver and muskrat. She believed that to be happy and healthy, one had to be active, a style of life she kept up almost to the day she died at age eighty-two in 1953.

When Wabiko, Juliette's father, was chief, the first language of a vast region of this country was Nishnabi. People identified as Nishnabi ranged from the Maritimes to the Prairies and from the Great Lakes to the sub-Arctic. According to Nishnabi history, the very name of this country, Canada, comes from the Nishnabi word, *Ca-da-yand*, which means literally "where we live."

It is easy to imagine how the newly-arrived immigrants of three hundred years ago might have come to know the land by that name. There is no record, however, of the time *Ca-da-yand* came into common use. Most likely, Champlain adopted that name when he first met with the Nishnabi (Algonquin). Well he might have asked, "What land is this?" In reply, he might have heard *"Ca-da-yand."* To the French settling along the banks of the St. Lawrence in those early days, the word became "Canayen." This mixture of language had its equivalent in the *metissage* (mixture of blood) of the newly-

indigenous cultures, leaving the survivors easy prey to the European invaders who circled the globe. In this chapter, I will show how that devastation nearly wiped out the Natives of Kipawa territory and compare this with the effects of the epidemics elsewhere in Canada.

The epidemics among the indigenous people in Kipawa were catastrophic. Elaine Allen Mitchell's book, *Fort Timiskaming and the Fur Trade*,[1] describes some of their effects. Mrs. Mitchell takes her information from the archives of the Hudson's Bay Company and the North West Company. Fort Timiskaming was the principal trading post of the upper Ottawa River serving the territory of Kipawa. In her book, Mrs. Mitchell deals with the epidemics of 1817 as follows:

> An epidemic, of whose origin and nature Cameron[2] seems to have been ignorant, raged amongst the Indians. It lasted throughout the winter and Cameron twice mentioned sending out medicine to gravely ill Indians, a number of whom died. One of his favourites, "Plum blanc," though ailing, survived to see another spring; he died shortly afterwards.

Mrs. Mitchell recorded another epidemic that struck the Metawagamingue Indians in a region to the north in 1819. This was " 'a kind of Rheum and Flux,' as Cameron described it." She speculates that since measles and whooping cough were prevalent in other parts of the country and since Cameron "apparently did not recognize any of the usual symptoms, it may have been a virulent form of influenza or perhaps tuberculosis." She goes on to say that:

> ... reports of Indian deaths continued to come in, among them that of a hunter whom Cameron mourned as "the best Indian belonging to this post." Concern for his trade mingled with the distress he felt for his flock. Dead

---

1. Toronto: University of Toronto, p. 110.
2. Angus Cameron, agent and partner in the North West company, Temiskaming district, during the first half of the 1800's.

Indians hunted no more and widows and orphans were apt to become a "troublesome" charge on the post.[3]

Two more disasters struck Fort Timiskaming in 1843. One was an epidemic of tuberculosis, the inevitable product of white-Indian contact. According to Mrs. Mitchell, the disease:

> ... appeared at Grand Lac in 1843, immediately affecting recruitment of crews for the post's transport, and by 1847 had spread all over the Temiskaming district. The disease was not simply one of the lungs but also took the form of scrofula, or King's Evil (tuberculosis of the bone and glands).

She goes on to say that Indians died by the dozens in "horrible circumstances, many, from weakness, lying where they fell." Their sores were "prey to maggots and themselves, 'food for the worm when alive,' " as James Cameron[4] observed. Such a painful state, he declared, he had never before witnessed.[5]

Coupling with disease was fire, which swept the Temiskaming area in 1846. Writes Mitchell:

> The summer of 1846 turned out to be one of the hottest on record and forest fires raged all over the James Bay country, not only burning the woods but the earth as well. Among the areas most severely affected was Lake Timagami, where the fire overran most of the Indian lands, and where for the future little could be expected in the way of furs.

She adds that starvation followed the destruction of the game that resulted. This, together with the intense heat, weakened the victims resistance to the epidemics even further. She quotes James Cameron as writing to his father, "Alas, for Temiscamingue. Its band of fine

---

3. *Op. cit.*, p. 112.
4. James Cameron, the nephew of Angus Cameron, also worked for the North West Company.
5. *Ibid.*, p. 192.

Indians are at an end." The Indian deaths also added to the decline of the fur trade in Temiskaming. Mitchell notes that:

> Although the decline in returns was partly due to the reduced price of beaver and the Company's discouraging its being hunted, the principal reason, he explained, was sickness among the Indians, who were still dying at an alarming rate. If things went on as they were, the Fort would be depopulated. Fortunately the epidemic reached its peak that summer of 1849, although it was to persist for some years longer.

One wonders at the utter despair and the dreadful feeling of being attacked by an unknown enemy; and the weakness, the suffering, the starvation, and the demoralization that must have carried from one generation to the next. As recent as my childhood days, people, indeed entire families, lived in seclusion, not allowing anyone to enter their home for fear of disease. Mitchell describes this feeling:

Margaret Rogers, one of the children who escaped the epidemics of the 1800's, lived to see five generations of her children. In her lifetime she cooked many meals in the outdoors in this fashion.

---

6. *Ibid.*, pp. 192-193.

Curiously, the epidemic temporarily affected the popularity of the priests and was probably responsible for the state of affairs at Moose Fort during the summer of 1849, about which Laverlochère[7] had complained to Sir George.[8]

James Cameron comments that the Indians themselves noticed that those who attended the services and took the pledge to abstain from drinking sickened and perished in greater numbers than those who kept their old faith and drank once or twice a year. Mrs. Mitchell adds that this situation:

> ... in James's opinion, was due to the fact that the Christian Indians collected at Fort Timiskaming and lived on imported provisions, while the pagans stayed mostly on their own lands, visiting the post only at long intervals. He was nevertheless finding it difficult to persuade his Indians to accept goods or provisions in place of liquor.

She quotes James as saying that unless the use of liquor was stopped entirely, he could not see how he could keep them from it.[9]

Today, no one remembers the 1847 epidemic; still, a few oldtimers remember the tuberculosis tragedy around the turn of the century and the influenza that claimed many more lives in 1918. The tuberculosis outbreak of 1847 probably persisted into the 1900's, contributing to the high mortality rate caused by the influenza epidemic of 1918. That the tuberculosis epidemic might have left the people of Kipawa vulnerable to the second infection is reflected in the death rate among the Natives of Kipawa as compared to that of the non-Natives in the same area.

Two villages in the territory point up this occurrence. Hunter's Point included among its residents four families of whites, eight of Métis, and two of Indians. Although there were no fatalities among

---

7. Laverlochère: Father Nicholas Laverlochère, Oblate missionary at Fort Temiskaming from 1844-1851.
8. That is, Sir George Simpson, Governor of the North West Company at the time.
9. *Ibid.*

Michel and Catherine Shene seen at their hunting cabin, on Saseginaga Lake in the 1920's. They had three daughters and five sons. All five sons died from tuberculosis and smallpox in their childhood years. Mr. and Mrs. Shene reached their eighties before passing on.

the white families, one person died among the Métis and six died among the Indians.

The other village, called The-Mouth-of-the-Moose, contained ten Indian families, one of which was of mixed blood. The mixed-blood family was the only one to survive. Except for five adults and three children, the other families were wiped out. The mortality ratio of these two villages indicates how deadly influenza was to the pure Native.

In general, Native people from Labrador to the Yukon tell the same story of epidemics. When I was an executive member of the Native Council of Canada from 1974 to 1975, I visited Native communities throughout the country. Everywhere, the story was the same. Elders of each community told me of diseases that took eighty to ninety per cent of the population.[10]

Two elders in Kipawa who remember the tragedies early in the century recalled those events. One is Frank Robinson, eighty-two, a Métis who lived at Wolf Lake, a trapping village and site of a trading post, where subsistence farming and lumbering also began.

---

10. For a dramatic instance of population decline, that among Natives of British Columbia, see Duff, Wilson, *The Indian History of British Columbia*.

"Old Mathias" was one of those people who lived through tragic times. He had one son who survived, and he never spoke of the children he lost, as far as anyone can recollect. As was customary for the times, his Christian name became the family name of his son and stepson. That name Mathias was all he ever needed and he was known affectionately as "Old Mathias," till the day he died. Old Mathias was a man of marvellous good health. It was said that in his seventies it was not unusual to see him running along behind his dog team, on his way to or from his hunting grounds. Despite his advanced years he could carry a quarter of moose like a young man. This picture was taken when he was eighty-four. He died at Wolf Lake twelve years later.

I asked him to recall the epidemic that hit Wolf Lake.

Q. Frank, a little while ago you mentioned that a lot of people died from consumption or TB?

A. Ya, a lot of people died from that.

Q. How many people do you think died?

A. That's damn hard to say, I was a young lad then. I remember people coming to tell my mother of

18

families dying all over the bush. Everybody talked Indian then.

Q. Did you ever try to figure out how many died?

A. I don't remember anybody ever saying how many died. When they talked to my mother it was about the people who were left, the kids.

Q. There were villages too. What about them?

A. Ya. Grassy Lake and Brulé, they were wiped out.

Q. What size were those villages?

A. Oh, I don't know, maybe ten, twelve families, each. They had little farms. I used to see them people coming to Young's store in Wolf Lake—scared—everybody was scared. My mother told me not to go near them.

Q. Had you been to those villages before they were wiped out?

A. No.

Q. How about after?

A. A few years after I saw those places. There was nobody living there. The houses were starting to fall apart. They were pulled apart too, by trappers and lumbermen passing through, to make fire with.

Q. Why did the people leave their homes?

A. Everybody believed in the *Manido Wig-u-Wam* then. That's a bad spirit like a devil or something. They thought the Manido Wig-u-Wam come into their homes to kill them. Nobody ever lived there again.

Q. When did the smallpox hit then?

A. A few years later. Around 1910 I guess. Not so many died then.

Q. How big were those villages?

A. Oh, about ten or twelve families each.

Q. How did you know about the disease?

A. Everybody talked about them. Scared, too!

Paddy Reynolds also lived at the time of the Spanish Influenza epidemic. When the epidemic struck The-Mouth-of-the-Moose, a little village on Dumoine Lake near Moose River, his father ran a trading post. I asked Paddy to recall what happened then.

Q. Paddy, what do you remember about the village at the Mouth-of-the-Moose?

A. Lots of people die time of the damn flu, there you know. That time the people pretty near all die, that time. Not too many left, just us.

Q. Just one family?

A. No, John-George too you know, Pawda's family too, you know, all the rest die.

Q. How many families were there?

A. About ten you know. Lots of people come there. I remember the flu, me.

Q. You were too young to be working, digging graves and such?

A. Ya, I was too young.

Paddy Reynolds, the only survivor today of the village at the mouth of the Moose River, on Dumoine Lake, which was destroyed by the 1918 influenza epidemic. He is pictured here with one of his grandchildren in the Kebaowek Reserve, Kipawa, where he now lives.

Q. Who was doing all the work to look after those people who were sick?

A. My dad and my brother, you know. We didn't get sick, us. There was me and Joe and my dad and my grandmother, you know. My dad was making coffins, my brother too and John-George too. Everybody worked a little bit too, you know, bring some wood in. Bring water in too. Bring food too. My grandmother used to cook food, take it over to sick people, that's what I used to do. Lots of people, he die way back in the bush too. Oh, quite a few families, they die up there you know. Just one woman didn't get sick. They call her Mrs. Brazeau, you know. She looked at all the sick people. Just two kids got all right, just two got better, all the rest

21

die. They were way past Sucker Lake. After they got a little better, then they come down to Mouth-of-the-Moose. That time my dad had a trading post there. They come down before freeze-up, oh, can hardly walk, them people. Just one woman not sick. Tough times you know.

Q. So what happened to the houses at the Mouth-of-the-Moose?

A. Oh, people tear that down, you know, make wood with them. Trappers. They were nice houses too, you know, all square timber houses. We used to have big house those days too, upstairs. Trappers, he make wood with that.

The diseases were most deadly to the pure Indians. This phenomena might be explained by the fact that before the invasion of the Americas, Europe had gone through three hundred years of Black Death[11] (also known as bubonic plague) and its attendant diseases. The survivors became immune to highly developed strains of these diseases. Consequently, the strains that were brought to the Americas were of the most deadly variety. This might also explain the lower mortality rate of the mixed-bloods—acquired genetic resistance.

As devastating as Black Death may have been, it paled in contrast with the death rate and psychological shock to Native America, enduring wave after wave of new diseases. Generation after generation was decimated. Although survivors gained a degree of

---

11. According to the *Chambers Encyclopedia* (New Revised Edition, 1973), human plague has been known for some two thousand years, if not more. Half the population of the Roman Empire was wiped out by a great epidemic (pandemic) lasting from A.D. 542 to 594. Another pandemic arose in the fourteenth century in eastern Asia, then spread to Asia Minor, Arabia, Egypt, northern Africa, and Europe, reaching England in 1348. This so called Black Death destroyed some twenty-five million people in Europe and over half the population of Great Britain. Other epidemics swept the near east and Europe from the fourteenth to the seventeenth centuries. This included the Great Plague of London in 1665, which wiped out sixty thousand out of a population of 450,000.

One of the residents of the village at the mouth of the Moose River on Dumoine Lake prior to the destruction of that village by the flu in 1918.

immunity to one disease, it was often followed by another that was even more devastating. Children grew up to be infected by their parents. While the plague at its height carried off half the population in Europe, in the Americas each new disease had the potential of yet another Black Death.

In their book *Indians and Other Americans*, Harold E. Fey and D'Arcy McNickle estimate that in 1492 there were 900,000 living in the territory now the United States. They reached the figure by:

> . . . a careful searching of the journals and reports of explorers, traders, religious missionaries, and official

commissions of varying degrees of veracity. We read accounts of how, when men first entered a long-sealed tomb and admit the outside air, objects shatter before they are touched.

This was no less true of the aboriginal populations on European contact. They go on to say that:

> ... the pilgrim fathers landing on the Massachusetts coast found what seemed to be an empty and deserted land, though they could discern fields that had been planted to corn in the recent past. Later they were told that a plague (possibly scarlet fever) had destroyed the people in great numbers, and the Englishmen realized that the New England Indians had already been in contact with Europeans.

This tendency for disease to sweep through Native populations occurred throughout North America. Fey and McNickle conclude that "so severe was the population decline that by 1880, if census counts are to be relied upon, the Indians numbered about 250,000. Out of this shadow of threatened racial extinction was fashioned the phrase "vanishing red man."[12]

Over the past four decades I have watched with interest the varying guesses of what the Native population might have been at the time of Columbus's first visit. Researchers from the government and various academic disciplines have estimated the Native population of that time to be equal to the Native population of the present day. A major factor in such an estimate would have to be the number of people wiped out by those diseases. Such estimates are not possible.

It must be remembered that the early fur traders and missionaries rarely strayed far from the main trade routes. In fact, having established forts and trading posts, they invited the Native people to visit them. The vast hinterland was unknown to Europeans. Consequently, the death and destruction viewed from the fort or post was only the tip of the iceberg of human suffering.

---

12. Harold E. Fey and D'Arcy McNickle, *Indians and Other Americans* New York: Harper and Row Publishers, Inc., pp. 9, 10.

The Native people at present are probably at a stage of recovery comparable to that of the population of Europe after the Great Plague, in the seventeenth century. How long it may take for the indigenous people to regain their precontact state of physical, social, economic, and spiritual well-being will depend on a number of basic factors. Many of those factors are those over which they have little control.

If the death toll among the Native population reached such high proportions, then one must ask how healthy the indigenous people were before their contact with Europeans. Here, in part, is a statement by Raymond Obomsawin, published in *The Canadian Nurse,* October 1978:

> The precontact Indian people of this continent were extremely healthy and virile. Out of over 30,000 recognized diseases only 87 were known to exist, and then very rarely, amongst the Indians of North America. We lived in freedom from hospitals, insane asylums, police forces, and prisons. We were among the healthiest people on earth; we are now among the unhealthiest.[13]

That our ancestors practiced a healthy way of life harmonizing with the natural environment is clear from letters that the colonizers wrote to their superiors in Europe during the seventeenth century (National Archives of Canada). The newcomers, especially the missionaries, abhorred the Native "heathen" practice of frequent bathing in the lakes and sweat lodges. Reports abound of the Europeans admiration of the fine physical specimen living in this "new" land. One letter tells of several "Indians" taken to the Royal Court of England to demonstrate their strength and agility (there is no record of their return).

Those who survived the epidemics invariably lived to a ripe old age. The longevity of the survivors must be accepted as truly indicative of the excellent state of health among the Native people prior to the arrival of the Europeans. Yet, a sort of paradox developed among the survivors. Naturally, because children are that vital link in the continuation of life, the people mourned more for the

---

13. *The Canadian Nurse,* p. 8

children lost to the epidemics than any other. Yet they were the hardest hit.

Today's epidemics are different. Death no longer strikes on a massive scale as it did in the past. The results are more subtle, and the causes are alcohol, poor nutrition, unemployment, and economic and social injustice. This syndrome of self-destruction is surely based on alcohol.

This flow of alcohol has indirectly caused the breaking up of families. Nationally, there are now approximately forty-five thousand Native children estimated to be under the care of Children's Aid Societies in one way or another. Is this not the greatest shame that any people could endure? Combined with this has been a loss of respect for the elders, from whom most of the children of civilized societies gain their wisdom and guidance. Weaving a tortuous web through almost every case of family breakdown, child neglect, violence, suicide, accident, and crime is the venomous flow of alcohol.

This problem has been obvious in Kipawa, a village of 450. Last winter, there were two snowmobile fatalities and several acts of violence related to the use of alcohol. I expect that the incidence here is not far from the national average for Native communities. Is alcohol the problem, or might it be the outward manifestation of a feeling of powerlessness brought about by repeated generations of corrupted, insensitive colonial manipulation as is demonstrated by the present attempted land-grab in Kipawa? Or might the weakness for alcohol also be related to physical and mental anguish of centuries of repeated epidemics? Both evils inhibit the Native psyche today. Nothing can be gained by dwelling on past tragedies, however. If gains are to be made, Native people must stand up for their rights, set their own goals, and demand that governments cease their colonial dominance and biased management of resources.

The problem of alcohol in Kipawa, or any other Native community in this country, will not be lessened until we begin to solve the social, economic, cultural, and identity problems. Many of the factors of change are government controlled, and colonial governments as a rule are self-serving. It is always an uphill battle to get governments in this country to recognize problems and to act on principle where the indigenous people are concerned. That is a fact of life that will not change. Therefore, the people themselves must learn the use of power and exercise it, in order that their children might some day live with respect, dignity, and equal opportunity.

If fighting government is a long-term battle, there is at least one problem the people can tackle immediately: nutrition. Over the generations we have acquired poor diet habits by eating too much sugar, sweets, soft drinks, starches, and other junk foods. Junk foods are made up mostly of grease, starches, and sugar, all lacking nutritional value and all lending to obesity. That a fat body is a healthy body is a mistaken assumption; obesity generally reflects eating too much, eating the wrong foods, or failing to exercise enough; often a combination of all three may be responsible. Choosing good food when shopping is an exercise of common sense: choosing fruit instead of sweets; vegetables instead of starches; and lean meat and fish instead of fat meat.

It goes without saying that poor nutrition eventually leads to poor physical and mental health. The Canadian Association in Support of Native People published a brief summary regarding the causes and effects of poor nutrition among Natives. Table 3.2 lists some of the more common illnesses caused by poor nutrition:

Table 3.2 Malnutrition-Caused Diseases

Acne	Diabetes	Infant Diarrhea
Anemia	Ear Infections	Obesity
Dental Decay	Gall-Bladder Disease	Rickets

The same organization lists some of the reasons for poor nutrition, as follows:

1. Overconsumption of sugar, sweets, and soft drinks, which contribute to obesity, diabetes, and tooth decay.
2. The substitution with poor-quality store foods such as black tea, processed meats, and sugar-laden desserts for game meats, wild berries, bush teas, and other wild foods.
3. Substitution of bottle-feeding for breast-feeding. For nutritional value to infants, mother's milk is still unsurpassed.
4. High consumption of black tea. Black tea contains tannic acid and other elements which destroy certain nutrients.

5. Underconsumption of fresh fruits and vegetables, the major sources of folic acid and vitamins A, and C. Fresh fruits and vegetables are especially needed where the traditional sources of these vitamins (berries, bush teas, and raw meats) are not consumed.

The availability of wild meat, fish, and berries is certainly one of the underlying issues in Kipawa. The loss of family hunting territories has taken away the traditional sources of natural foods. Natural foods that were the sustenance and vitality of a people for thousands of years are now considered the inheritance of sportsmen.

How have historians treated this disaster, past and present? At best, the record is spotty. That the history books of Canada pay scant attention to the epidemics visited upon the indigenous people may have been due to ignorance on the part of the explorers and missionaries. They may not have known that they carried those diseases. But that is hardly any reason for our history to remain distorted.

Take, for example, the manner in which history books relate the destruction of the Huron nation on Georgian Bay. The horror of that sudden and extremely tragic death of a nation is told as a story of heroism and martyrdom of six Jesuit priests. For example, one historian writes that "no Indian brave ever met the tortures of the enemy with more iron courage than he. For fourteen hours they tortured the gentle Father Lalement, until death released him from his agony."[14] For whatever reasons the priests accepted death, they were only six compared to the almost thirty thousand Huron who succumbed to the diseases that the priests and their kind brought. Typical of the biases that Canadian historians display is this excerpt:

> Champlain had not been long in Quebec before he had missionaries brought out, for one of his fondest dreams was that the Indians might be converted to Christianity. The task of carrying the gospel into the Huron country was entrusted to the Jesuits, a strong and powerful order

---

14. Aileen Garland, *Canada, Then and Now*, (Toronto: MacMillan of Canada, 1959), p.65.

of monks. The story of their mission is a proud and glorious page in the history of Canada. They endured incredible hardships, and many of them sacrificed their lives in their heroic attempts to save the souls of the Indians.

None of the missions the Jesuits established in the Huron villages south of Georgian Bay became permanent settlements like Montreal. The missionaries had only a few years to work before the Huron villages were wiped out by the fierce and savage Iroquois.[15]

The writer ignores the true cause of the destruction of the Huron nation—disease. Jesuit intrusion led directly to the smallpox, influenza, dysentry, and other epidemics that eliminated the Huron. Although in one winter priests may have fed six thousand Huron, the numbers of that nation dropped from thirty thousand to twelve thousand in a single generation. If this was a "proud and glorious page" in Canada's history, then the annihilation of the Huron was a "proud and glorious" event. For that matter, imagine the bewilderment of a Mohawk (Iroquian) child subjected to this piece of propaganda in the same book: " 'My pen,' wrote the Father Superior of the mission, 'has no ink black enough to describe the fury of the Iroquois.' "[16] Not a single mention is made in that book of the epidemics that sealed the doom of the Huron. Why do today's historians still echo those self-righteous notions of religious zealots who presumed their right to "saving" Indian souls?

Ignorance and racism as expressed in this manner may have been the norm for the seventeenth century, but why do we tolerate such phoniness in the teaching of our children today? As a rule, history has been purposely biased against indigenous peoples; little else can be expected of the internal colonial policies of this country. It is the Native child who suffers the brunt of this distortion. Small wonder that many of these young people drop out before completing high school. The bright and the sensitive are quick to perceive the phoniness of Canadian history and soon lose interest in attending schools that distort such accounts.

---

15. Garland, *op. cit.*, p. 64.
16. *Ibid.*, p. 67.

In all fairness it must be acknowledged that some provincial education ministries, perhaps influenced by a budding commitment to human rights in Canada, have realized the extent of racial prejudice of Canadian historians and have taken some steps to modify some of the ultra-colonial distortions of the past. But is this enough?

The Ministry of Education for Ontario, with the cooperation of the Department of Indian Affairs, has published a resource guide titled *People of Native Ancestry* for the guidance of teachers at the intermediary level for teaching Native Studies. Although no doubt this is a step in the right direction, there are two interwoven aspects of teaching that might still impede the truth: the reference material and the teacher.

Canada, Then and Now, the text that is referred to in this chapter is still being used as a reference book by some teachers in dealing with the Iroquois, the martyrs and the demise of the Huron Nation. In reviewing four other Canadian history texts[17] presently being used from the intermediary to the college level published in the decade between 1960 and 1970, I find that three made no mention of the epidemics as at least a contributing factor in the annihilation of the Huron Nation. One conceded that, "A small pox epidemic, for instance, drastically reduced the Huron population in the early 1600's." Essentially all four attributed the death of the nation to the fierce Iroquois.

Teachers who are indoctrinated with these falsehoods in childhood are inclined to look to reference material that enforces these ideas and so once again it is passed on to the unsuspecting young.

There will be a residual effect of these racially biased distortions of history for some time to come unless there is a positive move on the part of the legislative, judicial, and educational institutes of this country to set the record straight both in the historic and contemporary sense.

It is generally thought that the epidemics among Native people

---

17. These history text books were: *Northern Destiny*, John S. Moir and Robert E. Saunders, (J.M. Dent & Sons Limited, 1970), p. 70; *Land of Promise*, John L. Field and Lloyd A. Dennis, (The House of Grant [Canada] Ltd., 1960), pp. 82-84; *Fair Domain*, George E. Tait, (Ryerson Press, 1960), pp. 102-105. *The Canadian Experience*, Moir and Farr, (Ryerson Press, 1969), pp. 42-43. The first, *Northern Destiny*, made the reference to the epidemics.

were caused simply by the innocent encounter of one group of people, immune to their own diseases, with another lacking such immunity. This spread of disease was not always innocent or accidental, however. We know that germs were part of the war arsenal among the unscrupulous in both Canada and the United States. During the Pontiac rebellion, Colonel Jeffrey Amherst, the Commander-in-Chief of the British army in North America issued orders to his field commander, Colonel Bouquet, to spread disease throughout the rebelling tribes by giving infected blankets to their Indian prisoners of war. This order was one of the earliest cases of germ warfare that is known and fully documented. Colonel Amherst's order reads as follows:

> Could it not be contrived to send the Small Pox among those disaffected tribes of Indians. We must on this occasion use every stratagem in our power to reduse them . . . you will do well to try to innoculate the Indians by means of blankets, as well as to try every other method that can serve to extirpate the execrable race.[18]

There is little doubt that the disease carrier was the most powerful weapon of colonization—greater even than guns and religion—in those areas of the world that had been, up until then, relatively free of disease.

Whether the spread of germs was intended or accidental it set the stage for easy colonization wherever Europeans landed. Their diseases generally wiped out the majority of the population and left the remainder so demoralized that they were eventually reduced to a state of dependency. The rapid spread and the deadliness of the epidemics convinced Native people that the diseases were somehow devil-inspired and in their weakened state the survivors became willing, albeit unknowing, victims of foreign influence and treachery. This permitted the invader, because of his immunity, to exploit the plagues by taking advantage of the people in a material and territorial

---

18. *The Conspiracy of Pontiac and the Indian War after the Conquest of Canada*, Francis Parkman. Vol. 2. (The Museum Book Co., Toronto, 1886, 10th ed.), pp. 35, 37, 39-40.

sense, and also in a psychological sense by pretending that he was favored by God with spiritual, racial, and cultural superiority—the use of bigotry to justify colonial enslavement. This attitude is still very much evident in the actions and public pronouncements of politicians, and in their debates on the rights and equality of Native people—the born-again colonizers.

The original people of this land were weakened, dispirited, and decimated by European disease, to a point where they had neither the energy nor the will to defend their lands. They were robbed of their heritage, dignity, and freedom. The steps necessary for the return of these rights will be determined by the level of civilization in this country. Canada espouses human rights internationally; she would indeed gain stature by adopting the same principles at home.

CHAPTER FOUR

Land Use and Ownership

Paugene was unusual among the Nishnabi. Most non-Natives think of "Indians" as hunters rather than gardeners, but Paugene, who was probably ninety-one when he died in 1919, had a vegetable garden at Depotie Lake that was the envy of everyone in the Kipawa territory. No one really knows how he started, since gardening was rare among the hunting families. Champlain did, however, record Nishnabi family gardens on Allumette Islands (near Pembroke) in the early 1600's. Paugene's example prompted a few other families to add vegetables to their wild diet and to store crops as a hedge against hunger in times when game was scarce. He reaped hay from his own clearing and wild hay from the marshes for the lumbermen whose horses dragged the first square timbers out of the bush around 1868. Hay was good barter for the metal tools and imported foods of the lumbermen.

Joe Depotie, the grandson of Paugene, taken in the late 1930's with his wife Beatrice and children. From the left they are Emile, Violet, Noreen, and Alex.

33

Richard Depotie, seventeen, youngest son of Joe and Beatrice, who lives with his mother in North Bay.

As lumbermen and other propertied individuals cleared virgin forests from the lakeside, game dwindled or shifted to other areas. The eventual disruption and destruction of animal, fish, and bird habitats by timber cutting, log-drives, and poachers, who came with the lumber camps, made it necessary for some families to turn to gardening for part of their sustenance. Little vegetable gardens appeared along lakeshores once the preserve of hunters: Wolf Lake, Grassy Lake, Ogascanan, Saseginaga, Hunter's Point, Brennan, and the southern shores of Lake Kipawa.

Many Nishnabi were loath to give up their life of hunting for the garden. The Creator, they believed, had seeded the land with moose, deer, beaver, fish, ducks, geese, and countless other game. He had provided plants, berries, and herbs for their use as food and medicine. Every season, even winter, brought something to eat, and all Nishnabi lived within a natural cycle of production. Gardens marked the surrender of a way of life that had begun with the dawn of their existence. This chapter will describe that way of life—how land was owned, and how people lived on that land.

***

In the old days, specific territories were the domain of each family. This did not mean they were "owners" in the sense understood today. Rather, the families were stewards of their hunting territory, having inherited the guardianship of the land from the generations that had preceded them from time immemorial. To the family fell the duty of conserving the animal and plant life on their territory, and so preserving that way of life for generations to come. These people formed what anthropologists call bilateral extended families. They were made up of the husband and wife together with the children of both sexes; these children might also be joined by their husbands and wives. Every family lived within a subsection of their hunting territory; every year, they moved to another site, allowing the old site to replenish itself with game and plant foods.

With the arrival of the Europeans came changes in the use and attitudes toward the use of the land, for there had been lawlike customs concerning property long before the white man had heard of the Americans. If, as historian and archaeologist, Clyde C. Kennedy states in his book *The Upper Ottawa Valley*,[19] the indigenous people returned to the Ottawa Valley more than five thousand years ago, then the laws recognizing the rights of individual kin groups to hunting territories had thousands of years to jell. Furthermore, these rights were not for purchase or sale. The Nishnabi man and woman joined with the lakes, the streams, the animals, trees, even the rocks to form a living whole, in which the Great Spirit, the Manitou, dwelled. Small wonder, then, that the Nishnabi hunter gave up his way of life to become a wage earner or even a farmer only when faced with starvation.

Although, from the time of the Royal Proclamation of 1763, the British Crown had recognized Nishnabi land rights, these rights were conveniently ignored by local settler governments. As if the individual extended family never had rights of its own, the Quebec government in the mid-1800's declared all land "open," paving the way for hundreds of European loggers, miners, settlers of all description to take over the land on the strength of a scrap of paper called land title.

Thus, by hundreds of scraps of colonial paper the livelihood, culture, and identity of a Native nation have been all but destroyed. Loggers by the thousands have torn out the forests, miners have dug up its soil and dumped sludge into its waterways, and governments have opened roads to all parts of the territory, exposing the heartland of the Nishnabi nation to the murderous squanderings of so called sportsmen and tourists. If European colonists accuse the Native of

---

19. Clyde Kennedy, *The Upper Ottawa Valley*, (Pembroke, Ontario: The Renfrew County Council), p. 61.

going crazy with the bottle, the Native can justly accuse the colonist of being drunk with greed. The evidence is a massive festering sore upon our land that continues to spread its cancerous tentacles under the supervision of alien governments obsessed with economic growth and worship of the false gods of the *Gross National Product*.

In the era when the indigenous family held responsibility for its land every lake, pond, stream, hill, and valley had specific animal, bird, and fish life that was known intimately and guarded by its human overseers. There were places where berries grew, where certain herbs flourished, and where plants and trees provided better teas and medicines than others. The children knew on which islands the moose and deer calved, where fish spawned, and when baby beavers would appear in the ponds. Their world of learning was the nature of things around them. Beavers and groundhogs were the most common pets, but bears, otters, and foxes responded to kindness as well.

The territory was home to the indigenous family. This was obvious in a very practical sense; there was neither warehouse, nor refrigeration. The land always provided fresh foods. The indigenous family relied on their land as the preservation of life for today, tomorrow, and their children's tomorrows. Small wonder that a people engrained to a practical way of living, attuned with nature's clock, later became wage earners only with difficulty. Thousands of years of living as an intricate part of the ecosystem of the land is not easily forgotten.

Each family arranged its camp site to suit its hunting patterns. Several factors influenced the choice of campsite: the swift water and shoals where fish run or spawn in the spring and fall, resting places of geese and ducks, or a cluster of small lakes, ponds, and rivers ideal for hunting and trapping game in the winter.

As a rule shelters were constructed of either dome or teepee-shaped frames covered with birchbark or animal hides. Occasionally, if a family were lucky enough to find a smooth rock face on the side of a rise, they would build a shelter by leaning poles against the rock face to form an enclosure. These semi-rock shelters were generally longer than they were wide. The fire was made against the rock wall, which reflected the heat and channelled the smoke through a hole in the roof. The shelter had an opening at one end which served as a door. With the introduction of steel axes, log cabins replaced these huts and lean-tos.

A young fellow and his pets. *(Courtesy of the Ontario Archives)*

This traditional way of life fit in well with the environment for the people accommodated themselves with the season, the weather, and the life-cycle and movement of the game they hunted. In winter the family worked together (or survived together, if the winter were especially severe), in hunting, fishing, and the pursuit of crafts.

Then, when spring came, they canoed to Grassy Lake or some other predetermined place to live for the summer. The location, a semi-permanent site, was free of mosquitoes and blackflies and rich with fish, game, berries, and herbs. Several of these favorable sites were located throughout the territory, and each year the Chief and Council chose the following year's location on the basis of the necessities of life it provided.

After a winter of isolation, romance was quick to ignite and so spring was a time for courtship and marriage. Spring was a time for dancing, singing, games, and storytelling. It was also a time for the spiritual leaders to communicate with the spirits; a practice known as *ko-sau-pa-jgan* (see pp. 44-50).

Life in the summer village, if temporary, was light and cheerful. It became a feast, a social celebration, a *Mardi Gras* in the wilderness. Men assembled to brag about their winter's catch, to discuss the latest in deadfalls or steel traps, to gamble, or to participate in

37

contests requiring strength and agility. It was a time for work. Life in the bush wore out the canoes, snowshoes, sleighs, and toboggans. They had to be replaced for ease of travel was a key factor in survival. Those brief summer months was the time to make and garner this equipment.

The women carried out their social and domestic duties as well; arranging marriages and other social events, gossiping, exchanging recipes, trading new ideas for using herbs, plants, bush teas, and medicinal mixtures.

Summer brought boundless activities to the children. Boys competed in wrestling, canoe and swimming races, and shooting contests with their bows and arrows. They travelled together on short trips to test and compare their skills of hunting, fishing, and exploring. The girls were equally enterprising in following up the skills of their mothers. They never strayed far from the camp, for that was a man's right, but they swam, played in the sun, and created games that imitated the chores of their mothers. They learned to fashion clothes from many different skins of animals, to sew a moccasin, to knit a snowshoe or a canoe seat, and to make baskets and art symbols with birchbark. Girls carried a greater responsibility for continuing the Nishnabi culture than the boys did.

Many families visited their friends and relatives in distant villages, requiring a canoe trip of a week or two. Other families ventured south to watch the many strange events taking place on the Ottawa River—and perhaps turn a profit. Lumber camps were sprouting all along the river and the owners often paid good prices for furs. The lumbermen were always happy to exchange store goods for fresh meat and fish.

The missionaries made their annual rounds during the summer to perform marriages, baptisms, and conversions. The Nishnabi received the missionaries with considerable ceremony and fanfare regardless of the fact that many of the villagers remained "pagan." Those scenes must have been delightful for the beach was lined with birchbark canoes and the teepees, whose colors of moose, deer, and bear hides, birchbark, and the occasional white canvas formed the background. A mixed forest, overshadowed and dominated by huge white and red pines completed the background. Everyone dressed in his traditional best: buckskin, furs, and the very latest styles from the Hudson's Bay Company. Rattles and drums filled the air while the shaman evoked the help of benevolent spirits.

Skulls of moose, deer, and bear were fashioned into crown caps, sometimes with horns remaining, to create ceremonial headdress. The skins of different animals were sewn over this skull form to create a variety of colors and to make individual designs of each one. One can imagine what a missionary thought, given his constant lookout for the signs of "paganism" and his mission to deliver his charges from the flames of Hell.

Always knowing somehow when the priest was about to arrive, the villagers made elaborate arrangements for his welcome. According to one story, the priest was told on his arrival that the shaman had visioned his canoe a few days previously, foretelling the day and the position of the sun on his arrival. The priest flew into a rage over this prophesy. From this experience the people learned that spiritual thoughts were best not shared with the priest. So it seemed, God lived in a book called a "Bible," and only the priest had one of these God-books. He preached that anyone failing to obey the word of God would burn in everlasting fire. Among the taboos the priest announced were lovemaking, dancing, swimming, and gambling. These things called "sins" would either put the victim into a temporary blaze until his soul burned pure, or into this place called Hell for all eternity. Endlessly, the missionary repeated that phrase "for all eternity." None of his flock understood the meaning of that phrase but it sounded so ominous, they told him only what he wanted to hear and so avoided his wrath.

Each year the scene was repeated. The moment the missionary canoe came into view every man in the village with a gun fired it off. A mad scramble followed amid the musical din of crying babies and howling dogs, to get the whole village canoe-borne. Soon, all the villagers were seated, gliding with fast-dipping paddles toward their visitor, their man of Heaven, to escort him ashore, where the elders met him.

As soon as the niceties were over there was a feast of the delicacies from the bush. One elder, recalling for me one such annual occasion many years ago, described the menu of that day. There was moose meat cut into small steaks and roasted over an open flame; there was also baked moose guts stuffed with marsh lily root and oatmeal, as well as boiled moose nose and brains. Beaver, boiled or roasted was also served. So was that special delicacy, beaver tail, which was tenderly toasted over an open fire. Fried muskrat quarters, duck and fish, each specially prepared, rounded off the complement of meat for the feast. Several wild vegetables from the marshes, along with preparations of bush and herb teas, garnished the feast. Many of these herbs are no longer in use; some have even been forgotten. Food from the trading post also formed part of the feast: bannock, a bread made of flour, lard, and baking powder, and sometimes sweetened with sugar or wild berries, was baked on wood embers; and beans, which were either boiled or baked in the sand.

As the country opened up in later years the arrival of the priest became less cause for a traditional celebration, partly because the priests discouraged "pagan" ceremonies, and partly because another tuberculosis epidemic around the turn of the century left little to celebrate . . . The opening of the region commenced in 1894, when the rail line of the Canadian Pacific Railway Company reached South Temiskaming.

From that time onward, farmers, lumbermen, foreign trappers, tourists, and other settlers poured into Kipawa territory.

The fur trade, missionaries, and lumbering all created changes that were now taking place. Although gradual at first, the changes accelerated after the turn of the century. Marriage between Native people and Europeans increased for two reasons:

1. The Native population had been nearly wiped out by the epidemics of 1890 to 1910, leaving women and children of many families to fend for themselves.

2. Increasing lumber operations brought about an influx of lumbermen.

Intermarriage with Europeans tended to weaken the family hunting structure. The Natives of mixed-blood were inclined to homestead and accept wage employment more than those who were not, and to stay in the village more. The European strains that combined with the original race of Kipawa were indeed varied; they included Scots, French, Irish, English, and Norwegian. The combination brought together more than just the blood mixture, it joined cultures and social ideas. It had a lot to do with the opening of schools and churches and it integrated bush life with village life, which had not existed until whites came along.

Families were able to remain in the villages thus created, while the men trapped. The village system made it possible, as time went on, for the men to be employed ever further afield in lumbering, guiding,

On the left is Cecile Antoine, who became Mrs. Endogwen and then Mrs. Moore. She is the great greatgrandmother of the Moores, Larivieres, and Boudrias, and further branches of those names.

On the right is Rose Hansen, nee Antoine, who married Anton Hansen, a free trader, in the 1880's.

These families lived in Hunter's Point. Their descendents are numerous and are found from coast to coast.

dam-building, fire ranging, prospecting, and other jobs that required men of the bush. The villages became the pivotal points of their regions. The vegetables, the livestock, and the part-time jobs were never quite adequate, however. Furs remained the source of stable income, while wild meat and fish remained the main sources of protein.

There was a close bond between the villagers and the hunting

Ti-Gus Boudrias, a lumberman, and his wife Nancy, nee Endogwen, and their first son Henry.

families; in fact every hunting family in the bush had relatives in the villages. It was partly this relationship that influenced many of the hunting families to move to the villages. The Church and School also used their influence in persuading the people to move to one central location. Eventually, even the hunting family became a village family, for when Pien-ose's family moved to Hunter's Point from Ogascanan in 1942 the family hunting tradition came to an end. Where families once shared the wonders, joys, and tragedies of nature together, men now trapped alone.

Finally, the family hunting grounds died through government legislation in 1947. In that year the licensed trapping system came into effect. It was the beginning of a system that split the Kipawa territory into numerous tiny traplines, most of which were allotted to people from outside the territory.

CHAPTER FIVE

Spiritual Beliefs

If there is anything that the so called communications revolution has given to the Native people of North America, it is a sense of spiritual unity. Thanks to radio, television, and the newspaper, a thread of common beliefs runs through to form the framework of Native spirituality throughout the continent. That common belief rests with the Great Spirit; the almighty Master who lives everywhere and in everything. This is the reason why the Native respects all forms of life, essentially all existence. Man is provided with a spirit for a lifetime; though the body dies, the spirit lives on. This comes close to the concept of reincarnation. Yet nowhere do Native beliefs express the idea that the spirit returns for another earthly life. The spiritual theory of our oneness with the Great Spirit and all that He created appears to be gaining credibility in today's world. Thanks to man's greed for wealth, we see the land ravaged and the great oceans poisoned nearly to extinction. Perhaps the time has come for the creation of new spiritual theories and beliefs stressing man's oneness with his planet if he is to survive.

As I was gathering legends of my people, one of the elders told me a myth of magical power that summarized this theme of oneness. Handed down for generations, the story ran as follows:

> A long time ago, in primeval times, people pure of heart and living in harmony with nature, learned to use special powers. All people had these powers, but only the ones who worked harder to purify the body and spirit became more gifted. They became the shamans, or teachers. These shamans could talk with the Great Spirit. It is said that when a shaman spoke to the Great Spirit, his voice blended with the vibrations of creation, which is the source of all power. When a chief shaman chose to use his power he could move huge objects without touching them, change the weather, cure the sick, locate and stop animals in their tracks, and send fish and birds into nets. He could envision events that were to happen in the future, or that happened in the past. One level that junior

shamans strove to attain was the gift of the magic arrow. It seems this came about when a particular shaman gained enough power to "will" his arrow to return, after having shot it. In effect, when he attained this power he needed only one arrow—the magic arrow. When one attained this gift it became known that the Great Spirit was pleased with his progress. The young shaman became a superior warrior, for never did he need to reach for another arrow; the arrow was always at hand. It is said that the Great Spirit took away these special powers because the people became greedy and selfish in using their power. They hoarded food and riches, crushed their enemies without mercy and turned their leisure time from a life of purification to one of lust and self-satisfaction. The chief shaman warned the people that they were on the wrong path; and if they did not return to a state of purity, they would be harshly punished by the Great Spirit. The people paid him no heed, for they had begun to believe that the powers were their own. As profound as their powers over nature had been, no less profound was their fate. In an instant, the Great Spirit stripped them of all their powers, of all their possessions, leaving them naked in the forests. They were told that they would now go through a long period of extreme hardship. They would have to relearn their lost skills of hunting to survive. Another race from far away would conquer them and would heap great hardships and indignities upon them. They would be inflicted with disease, injustice, and loss of spirit. Thousands would even give up life to seek refuge in the next world. After a long time, when the people have been sufficiently humbled, they would be allowed a chance to regain the power of magic. The magic of the *ko-sau-pa-jgan* is given to certain individuals as a symbol of that promise and a reminder that the power still exists and will some day return.

The Nishnabi word for the spiritual world is *ko-sau-pa-jgan*. It describes the "shaking tent" and other forms of conjuring. That word differs slightly from dialect to dialect, but it is in common use wherever there are Nishnabi-speaking people.

Romantics have written about *ko-sau-pa-jgan* and the more serious-minded have contemplated the concept. It remains unexplained to scientist and poet alike; yet, from the elders one hears that in the days of its prominence, *ko-sau-pa-jgan* was attended without fear or awe. Amazingly, many young people have now turned to the practice of *ko-sau-pa-jgan*.

Ko-sau-pa-jgan is a spiritual belief rooted in the myths and legends of this land. It is the power to evoke mysterious forces, expressed in mental and physical actions that defy explanation in terms other than spiritual. The power of invocation rests with a shaman. That spiritual practice was used throughout North America. Natives worshipped or beseeched the Great Spirit through meditation, fasting, and dancing. Most noteworthy was the Sun Dance of the prairie, which in a broad sense expresses *ko-sau-pa-jgan* in another form. The Sun Dance brought the plains nations together in a ceremony to worship and pay homage to the Sun. No comparable celebration has ever existed in this part of the country. The Sun Dance was responsible for bringing a concerted effort by the governments of Canada and the United States to ban all Native spiritual ceremonies. Both governments saw the continuance of such spiritual ceremonies as a hindrance to their power and control over the assimilation of the Native peoples.

In my childhood, only to mention shaking tents or arts of conjuring while attending school or church was akin to mortal sin. For Native children, this was difficult to fathom; how could anyone believe that spiritual traditions, which the elders held dearly, would bring down the wrath of God?

Fortunately, a few had preserved *ko-sau-pa-jgan* and a new generation is once again learning the ancient mysteries of their ancestors. The adherents of this revived spiritualism stand out because of their commitment to sobriety, self-respect, and faith, a confidence that the Great Spirit will give them the knowledge and wisdom demanded for leadership and a fruitful life.

Never having witnessed *ko-sau-pa-jgan*, I have no first-hand knowledge to relate. Being skeptical about religious beliefs, I take the view that if we believe in the Almighty, we must at least believe that all things are possible. So I listen with an open mind to the tales of conjuring; perhaps the natural spirit of the Americas will revive and prove to be more civilizing and enlightening than the multitude of foreign superstitions and dogmas, which have tried to destroy it. Salvation may be an indigenous quality after all.

Recently, I had the good fortune of meeting a man of his late twenties who is a recognized shaman. In appearance he is no different from the average Native of his age. He wore his hair below his ear lobes and dressed in the clothes most bush workers wear. What astounded me was the quality of his eyes; they were piercing. He seemed to create a feeling of magnetism, an aura of gentle, firm will. The everyday life of a shaman, he said, is one of chastity, of austerity, of abstention from alcohol and drugs in all forms.

Several of the elders whom I have known hesitated to speak about *ko-sau-pa-jgan*. Nevertheless, one old fellow, elated that the young have again become interested, made every effort to remember details of an experience he had had long ago. I do not attempt to use his own words, since his English was halting and some of his expressions would not be generally understood.

The tent that he described was actually a dome-shaped structure covered with birchbark. The shaman, he said, selected saplings of every variety available. Then he bent them to make a sort of igloo-shaped shelter, with their ends firmly anchored in the ground. Over these saplings the birchbark was sewn together with spruce roots so tightly that it was impossible to see through the seams. So far as my friend knows there was no particular time for performing *ko-sau-pa-jgan*. The shaman, it seems, goes by some inner signal. There are exceptions, such as emergencies when they use their powers to cure someone who is sick, or to counter the curse of another shaman.

When the structure is completed the shaman goes through a ritual with chants, then enters the hut. He stitches himself in, drawing the thread so tightly that there is absolutely no way of seeing through. He then begins to speak in a low voice. In a short time other voices are heard, many voices. My friend tells me that he was very young when he saw the performance; yet to him, that experience remains vivid to this day. He said that the chanting, the voices, even the trembling impressed him not nearly as much as the quiet serenity that encircled the camp afterward; everyone might as well have been part of the communion.

John-George, the shaman, had made several prophesies that day that later came true. He told one woman present that her sister, who lived further north in the Abitibi region, had died and that she would soon hear about it by mail. Mail was slow in those days, and a month passed before she received the letter. The letter confirmed that her sister had indeed passed away.

An elderly gentleman, a non-Native, told me another story. He had trapped and worked in the bush in the mid-Canada corridor from Quebec to British Columbia. A veteran of World War I, he was a worldly man with a critical understanding of life. When he witnessed this particular event, he was in Nemiscau, a Naskapi village and Hudson's Bay post located on the Rupert River ninety miles from James Bay. Hearing that a shaman there was preparing *ko-sau-pa-jgan*, he was skeptical, and so made it a personal challenge to prove it a farce. He dared not confront him openly, however. He had previously heard of the "shaking tent" in different parts of the north, but had always missed these opportunities to see the "show." This time was different; not having anything better to do, he decided to prove that it was all hocus-pocus. He said that he was still quite confident while the shaman chanted, . . . "it didn't sound like anything more than an old man grunting." Then for no reason that he could understand the hut and the ground began to tremble, while many voices began to echo from the hut. Yet no one was inside but the old man. "There were both male and female voices, high and low voices, and some that were shrill and coarse." All the conjuring, he said, was unnerving, and he at first wanted to run out of there. But, when he looked around and saw everyone taking it calmly, he regained his nerve. Danger or fear seemed to be the furthest thing from the minds of those village people. He could not even guess how long the ceremony may have lasted, for he seemed to be caught in as much of a spell as everyone else. Suddenly, the trembling and the voices stopped. The shaman seemed to have been tossed through the wall; there he was lying on the ground, completely exhausted, and trembling a little. The wall of the hut was torn; the hole was large enough for a man to have been thrown through, yet no one had actually seen him fly through the wall. In a few minutes he seemed rested and completely calm. He then proceeded to tell everyone what the voices had said, and the prophesies he had received during his communion with the other world.

My friend said that he was particularly happy with one prediction that seemed so absurd as to be impossible at the time. The shaman had told that a giant bird, unlike any bird the people had ever seen, would appear from the south on the third day after *ko-sau-pa-jgan*, then land on the lake. The result of this prediction, or lack or it, would be a good chance to test the whole affair, yet he couldn't help wondering about the voices. Could it be that they were using some sort of ventriloquism? He waited patiently for the third day. To his utter dismay, on the morning of the third day, from the south end of the lake, a bush plane appeared. To the Native people it was doubtless the fulfillment of the prophesy. To my old friend, who was close to ninety when he told me the story, it was indeed a puzzle. He had heard that planes were flying over the bushland but they had never penetrated this far north before. The shaman had no word for "airplane" and could never have known in advance that one was coming, but the "big bird" arrived on schedule. The old fellow concluded by saying, "I still don't know what to believe. The darn thing baffles me to this day."

One example was given me how the shaman's power was sometimes used for evil. This incident happened at Wolf Lake village, in the early part of this century. The descendants of many of the people involved still live in the region of Kipawa. Since some may consider the use of the family name harmful, I will mention only that of the shaman involved.

As the story goes, a pretty young girl had been promised in marriage to one of two suitors. It was late spring and marrying time. The missionary had arrived for his usual short stay, but the young man to whom the young lady had been promised had not yet arrived. In the meantime the other young fellow had persuaded the girl to marry him instead. The priest performed the marriage, then left. Shortly afterward the first young fellow arrived. Understandably furious that his beloved had married someone else, he sought revenge. He immediately found a shaman by the name of Pawda, and asked him to put a curse on the man who had taken his betrothed. Word of this conflict got around the village very quickly, and the people shrank in horror of what might happen to the newlyweds. The young man was struck down by an invisible hand and seemed to be in a death stupor. Quickly his bride summoned another shaman by the name of John-George to lift the curse. It is said that the conjuring of John-George took the form of a ball of fire that flew off in the direction of Pawda's camp. Although the young man recovered, he suffered from convulsions for the rest of his life. Pawda's power had been believed to be greater than John-George's. Nevertheless, though John-George was unable to completely counter Pawda's curse, he did save the young man's life.

This picture, which is also the cover picture of this book, is of Tommy Pierre, sitting. Standing from left to right is John-George, his wife Jeanapeph, Tommy's daughter Clara, and his wife Sarah.

49

Stories of the Windigo, Manitou, and other legendary spirits have faded with the passing of every elder. What sort of events, real or illusionary, brought about these tales? What is the force of magic that causes a hut to tremble when it is firmly anchored, or voices to echo from the enclosure? Certainly, many have witnessed these strange happenings. Were all the onlookers mesmerized into seeing the same vision? Did the shaman use sleight-of-hand; if he did, what was his motive? Even strangers were allowed to observe and participate, yet no one has ever detected trickery. Are these stories to be classed as folklore of an almost forgotten era, or are they the remnants of a power that once existed?

If one believes, as most religions purport to believe, that all things are possible in this Great Universe; that all conceptions of life and creation are the works of God—the Great Spirit—and that there are no limits to those divine powers, then is it not conceivable that such individual spiritual powers did exist, like the technology of another era? What would happen if individual magical powers were to become revived in today's world?

CHAPTER SIX

The Fur Trade

The fur trade was the first to bring about changes in the life-ways in Kipawa territory. First of all, the people began to depend less and less on the game on which they had subsisted and more on the goods they could purchase from the trading posts in return for their furs. Second, the family territories may have dated from that time. There is disagreement on that point. Whether the territories began before European contact or after, it is known that property rights attached to each territory included the fur-bearing animals living there. Therefore, although the people of Kipawa were not yet living in the villages, the fur trade began to attach the people of the bush to them.

These villages in turn were also a passing phase of history. During the past four decades the villages were gradually deserted and the bulk of their former inhabitants make up the present Kebaowek Reserve and the village of Kipawa. Some of the Indian and Métis families still bear the names of the original inhabitants of the traditional hunting grounds, while others have adopted names that comply with the colonial religious system of identification, and by intermarriage. *(See Map 6.1)*.

Kipawa village itself is located at the southwest tip of a land area stretching over eight thousand kilometers; most of the land is traditional hunting territory. This territory commences twenty miles south of Temiscaming on the Ottawa River, then runs east beyond Dumoine River to Ten Mile Lake. A dip of the line takes in Lakes Beauchene (Lac Beauchene), Spearman, Maganisipi, Caughnawana (*kwakwa'ni*), du Fils (Lac du Fils), and Russel.

South of this line was the hunting grounds of the Nishnabi of Mattawa, whose territories were on both sides of the Ottawa River above and below Mattawa. The Kipawa boundary line then goes north taking in the Dumoine Lake area, including Moose Bay and Yantiquay Lake. The lower portion of that line meets with the territory of those Nishnabi, whose traditional grounds were the watersheds emptying south; the main rivers being the Black and the Coulonge. From the upper end of Ten Mile Lake, taking in Moose Bay and Yantiquay Lake, the boundaries extend to the boundaries of the Grand Lake Victoria people.

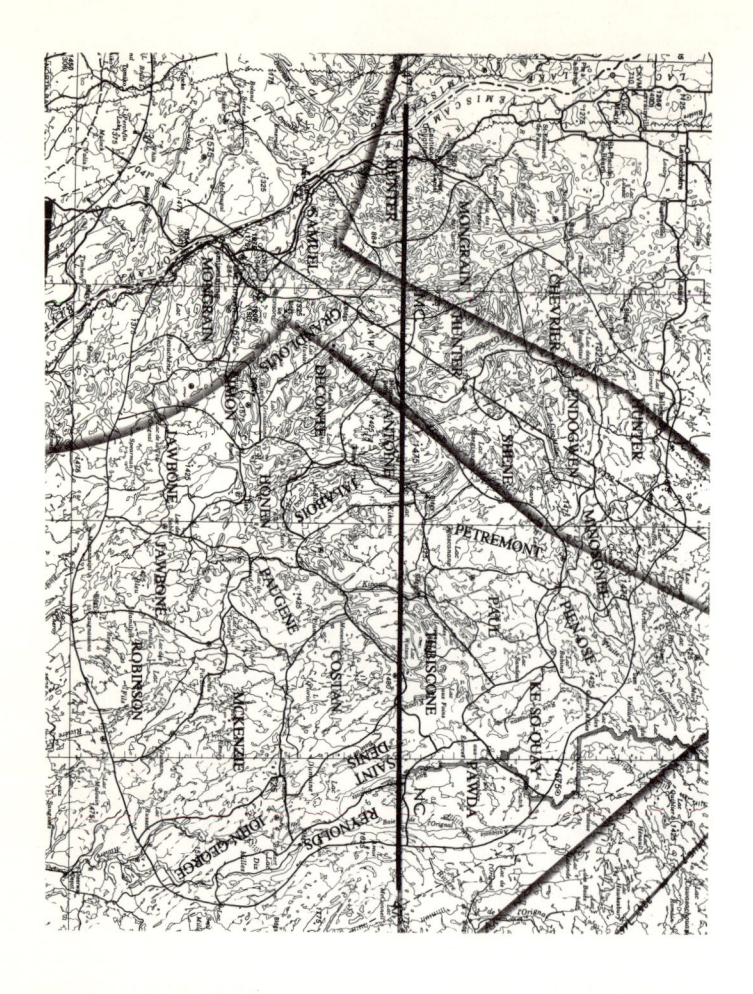

Map. 6-1. Kipawa Territory—Traditional Family Hunting Ground

Generally speaking, most of the indigenous names for the lakes, rivers, and land marks have been changed by government map makers and for this reason it is sometimes difficult to identify them;

A family outing on the shores of Dumoine Lake. This is the Reynolds family, Paddy and Arthur with their wives, mother and children. This Paddy is an uncle of the present day Paddy Reynolds of Kipawa. Arthur ran the mail from Dumoine Lake to the Ottawa River for the Eddy Lumber Company, in the early part of the century, and saved enough money to become an independent fur trader. He operated his trading post at the mouth of the Moose River until that community was destroyed by the flu in 1918.

for instance, the lake now known as Lac Beauchene due south of Lake Kipawa, was originally known as Obashing, meaning "lake of narrows."

From Yantiquay, the line follows the height of land to a point between Trout Lake and Winneway in a northwesterly direction, continuing on to the north side of Cross Lake. Along this portion the Kipawa Land borders on that of the Winneway Band. From there to the southwest it borders on the land of the North Temiscaming Band and follows the height of land between Devlin Lake and Sand Lake, the north side of Skunk Lakes and hence on to the watershed that feeds the northwest portion of Lake Kipawa, ending at that point on Lake Temiskaming where the Kipawa River empties.

Kipawa family territories crossed Lake Temiskaming but were disrupted in time by artificial barriers which deserve explanation.

***

The Ottawa Valley is the core of the eastern Nishnabi Nation. Like the veins of a giant leaf, the Ottawa River and its numerous tributaries created avenues of travel on a northwesterly, southeasterly axis close to four hundred miles in length and from one to two hundred miles in breadth at different points. The Ottawa watershed outlined the natural territorial limits of an indigenous people who saw themselves as a distinct nation. Thus, the Ottawa River boundary line which divides Quebec and Ontario is, strictly speaking, a Euro-Canadian division. It slices through the Nishnabi nation without respect for either the natural landform, or for family hunting territories.

Native family hunting territories were not divided by the river, but were in fact joined by it. When lumbering began on Lake Temiskaming in the 1840's family hunting groups were lodged in garden clearings at various locations along the waterway and generally controlled the immediate territory that emptied into the Ottawa from both sides near their home sites. The family names and sites were noted as follows: Jocko at the mouth of the Jocko river on the west side; Antisokan and Provencal at Opemican on the east side; Makinakose and Honen at Antoine's Point on the east side and Jawbone at the mouth of the Kipawa River on the east side. Other names were Yantiquay and Quaquani whose exact locations are lost to memory.

The provincial boundary line did not affect the descendants of those families until the 1940's when Ontario game wardens attempted to close the west side to people who lived on the east side of the river. Antoine Lariviere, a descendent of the Mackinakose family once recounted a brief exchange he had with a game warden over his right to hunt in Ontario.

> He picked up my traps and told me I couldn't hunt there any more. I told him that I had hunted there all my life and nobody could stop me. (Antoine was then eighty-six). I told him, if he touched my traps again I would shoot him—"at my age I don't care if I go to jail."

Other descendents and relatives of the original families continued to assert their rights to hunt both sides of the river until the 1950's. Individuals who hunted and trapped in contravention of provincial laws were Joe, Frank and Mike McKenzie, Mac Meness, Willie Michel, Henry Honen, Andrew Grandlouis, Louis Jawbone, Frank Robinson, and Baptiste Simon. They felt that the territory belonged to Kipawa families regardless of provincial laws.

The peoples who bordered the Kipawa group on all sides were Nishnabi and closely related. The differences in language between the groups were simply of dialect, as witnessed by the fact that they all spoke of themselves as "Nishnabi," a word which connotes "we," or "people," varying the pronounciation a little in different locations.

***

My first clear memory of the trapper's life was in 1933 when I was six years old. I remember going with my Uncle Frank across Wabiship Lake to Ostoboning. The purpose of our trip was to get a load of moose meat. He had several good huskies and it was a lot of fun to hang on to the sleigh through the bush trails and over the drifted snow on the lake. The trip to and from the site, where he had killed a couple of moose only a few days earlier, took only two hours, but to a six-year-old it was a journey to the ends of the earth.

Though it was a highlight of my young life, it was by no means the only one, for I lived the life of a trapper until I was sixteen years of age. We spoke of the hazards of bush existence and techniques of outsmarting animals as outsiders spoke of business and sports, for truly it was our business and our sport. It was so natural for us to hitch up a dog team in the winter, or to paddle a canoe in the summer to get somewhere, that when I started school the following year I was astounded to learn that the whole world didn't live that way.

No entertainment was imported in those days. The first radio that I listened to was bought by my Uncle George in 1934; it was some time before radio had much of an impact on most of the people in Hunter's Point. Story-telling, and mostly stories about trapping, hunting, or fishing, was the most popular pastime. Everybody talked about still-hunting moose and deer, trenching beaver and otter, or chasing fisher. All of these hunting techniques contained a built-in method of wildlife conservation.

There were different ways, for instance, of hunting moose. As a

55

rule, moose were not killed during the mating season. This was an innovation, considered exotic by tourists, so it became general practice reinforced by Canadian law. The most practical time to kill a moose for meat is in the winter when the freezer is the whole countryside. For the Native, that's when moose meat is most needed. One of the most effective methods of taking a moose in winter is the "still-hunt." The key to the still-hunt is stealth. The hunter generally knew where the moose were yarding, so when the time came to replenish his meat supply he waited for ideal snow and wind conditions, that is, when snow was fresh, temperatures had fallen below freezing, and winds were high. The high winds helped drown out any noises he might make, and so he approached the yard from the downwind side. A good hunter always examined the tracks to estimate the number of cows, calves, and bulls there might be. This was a way of determining which were the breeders. By taking only the nonbreeders the hunter ensured the herd would continue. Thus, the keenness of the hunter and his wisdom in selecting the right animal contributed to the conservation of his herd and the livelihood of his family.

"Holding moose" was another way of taking one. This method applied to bare-ground hunting in the fall. Basically all that was needed to hold a moose was a good little dog. Old bushmen used to point proudly to a favorite small husky and say, "That's a good dog; he can hold a moose." Strangers would be baffled by the thought of a thirty pound dog holding one thousand pounds of moose at bay. We used to tease the visitor for a few minutes before explaining. The dog, preferably a small one, is trained to find the moose and to bark at him without chasing him. With a small dog, moose get annoyed, but they will not run away, as they would if faced with a large dog. However, their total attention is taken up by the barking of the dog. To start such a hunt, the moose are usually located by paddling a canoe, with a dog, along the shoreline of a lake from which the wind is blowing. This is done until the dog gets a scent. When the dog gets the scent he growls, his back hairs stand on end, and he points upwind toward the moose. Let off on shore, the dog dashes into the bush, nose and eyes alert. He has been trained not to bark until he has reached the moose. The hunter waits until the barking has started, then walks to the moose yard and chooses the moose he will shoot. All the while, the dog carries on with his distracting bark.

Beside hunting moose, there were techniques for hunting other

Bringing in the moose meat. It wasn't so long ago that the land provided most of our food. Note the quarter of meat each man has on his back. They are Jean-Baptiste Brazeau, Andrew Young, Gordon Young, and Tony Brazeau. The tumpline backsack was typical.

animals. One was called "trenching beaver." The object was to scare beaver out of their houses and into the holes they had dug on shore as emergency shelters. This method worked best during the spring floods when ice was still on the lakes and the water level was rising, shutting off the breathing space between the ice and the water below. The water could also be raised artificially at times by breaking a dam that contained the water upstream from the beaver pond.

Briefly, the method was as follows. The hunter scared the beaver out of his house who, in turn, swam under the ice to one of the holes which had its entrance below the ice. With the help of a dog who sniffed out the beaver, the hunter cut the ice to the entrance of the hole, blocking its only escape. He then reached in, grabbed the beaver by a hind leg and pulled it out, clubbing it to death. If the beaver was too far in to reach, he dug a trench to get it out. Hence the name, "trenching beaver."

This method especially served to conserve the beaver. When he reached in, the hunter could usually feel the tail and so know by the size of his tail whether his quarry were an active breeder. The large and the small were taken while the young adults were spared to propagate the following year. Although this was obviously essential to the conservation of the animals, trenching beaver is outlawed today.

"Chasing fisher" was another technique that made hunting an adventure, although it did not involve so much chasing as following. Fisher are hunted from December to March, necessitating the hunter to use showshoes.

Chasing fisher probably started when the Native trapper first realized that fur companies paid more for fisher pelts than for those of other animals. The animal is worthless otherwise—the meat stinks. In the 1930's, the fisher was the most highly-prized pelt on the continent. A female pelt netted $150.00, truly a prize in those days when the ordinary workman made $30.00 a month if he were lucky. An agile animal capable of great endurance, the fisher may travel up to two days without stopping. If a trapper starts out on a fresh track, he always hopes that the animal will stop soon—there is no way a fisher can be run down. They can run circles around a man even in the fluffiest of snow in midwinter. Yet, when a trapper comes across a fresh fisher track, provided he has enough food in his packsack to hold him for a couple of days, he always follows it. If the trapper were lucky, two hours of travel might lead him to find the fisher holed up inside a big hollow dead pine, a sand hole on a hillside, or a rock cave. If he were not so lucky, it might take him a couple of days. When he finds the fisher, he invariably forces the animal out with smoke and shoots it as it emerges.

Several hunters like to recall the days they chased fisher. According to one story, one hunter trailed two fishers for three days before catching them. He then returned to the tent, showing his partner his prize and announcing he was returning home to Hunter's Point, a distance of twenty-five miles, that night. His job was done. If there is a moral to this story, it is that trappers were anything but fat and unhealthy. Who, today, would snowshoe for three days, sleeping in the open every night, then walk another twenty-five miles home?

When I think of the fur trade now, my thoughts return to the

In the old days dogs were the most valuable of animals. As hunters, as companions, able to haul supplies under the harshest conditions of winter, there was no equal to the bush dog. In the days before the advent of the snowmobile a good dog team was a trapper's proudest possession.

Hunter's Point of my childhood. The spring of the year was the most active time for hunting. It was the spring-hunt that created all the stir. The fall had its moments of excitement but winter was ahead and it was going to get colder before it got warmer. So, spring was the most pleasant part of the year for the trapper; he had the summer to look forward to.

Spring comes to the bush land amid a great flurry of excitement in the animal kingdom. Even before the ice has opened on the rivers and lakes, the landscape is bathed with the March sun and April showers. The beaver, the otter, and the muskrat begin to poke in and out of the holes and cracks that appear as the melting spreads its web along the lakes and rivers. Later, the ducks and geese begin to swarm in, and the trapper welcomes the change in his diet.

In those days, as now, beaver was the principal catch. Beavers multiply quickly, their meat is nutritious and tasty, and the market for the pelt is stable. For those reasons beaver was the main item of the fur trade from the beginning.

In Hunter's Point during those years, hunters paddled into the villages from all directions in their canoes laden with furs during the second or third week of May. Although some individuals owned Johnson and Evinrude motors, they usually left them behind for the spring hunt, because everything had to be hauled over the snow before break-up. Usually there were two men to a canoe, but families who spent the winter in the bush used larger canoes. These family groups still trapped in the traditional manner.

Charlie McKenzie as a fur buyer.

The trappers usually took their furs to either of two stores or trading posts. One, owned by Archie Perrier, was located at the narrows where Isaac Hunter, who gave Hunter's Point its name, cleared land and built the first house. The other trading post was owned by Garfield Jones; it was located at the upper narrows.

The furs usually came in large canvas-covered bundles. The pack was a tent held together by a tumpline or portaging strap. There wasn't much bargaining over the price of furs, for both traders had proven their honesty over the years. Often a trapper would have been grubstaked (provided with supplies) for the spring hunt by one or the other of the traders, so there was an unspoken obligation to sell to that trader.

One of the most formidable trappers of those times was one Jimmie Hunter. He was called "Old Jimmie," not only because he was getting on in years, but also because he had a son known as "Young Jimmie." He was a large man with a booming voice; in his youth he had broken many of the records for snowshoeing to different parts of the territory. He also had a knack for breaking beaver bones. This was a test of strength for the hands and wrists, which was popular amongst the bushmen. The object of the contest was to break the thigh bone of a large beaver. The bone was stripped of all meat and fat, and then dried to make it fit for gripping. It was grasped in both hands by the contestant and with a twist and snap of the wrists, the bone was broken, that is, if the contestant had the strength. It is said that Old Jimmie would stand around and watch the younger men struggle to snap the bones, then, faking annoyance, he would grab the bones and snap them one after another.

It was during one of his final years of trapping that Old Jimmie dropped in to see Archie Perrier to obtain provisions for the year. He announced to Archie that he would get one hundred beavers in the winter ahead. Now that was a rosy goal for even a young man, let alone a man past seventy! The word went out that the old man had gone into his second childhood. Everyone shut up when he finished the spring hunt with a count of ninety-nine beavers.

Old Jimmie's life experience had been broad and varied. As a young man he guided Hudson's Bay Company canoes from Lake Temiskaming to Grand Lake Victoria. He had worked with the lumbermen when they first entered the area. He even helped colonizers settle on his hunting grounds.

In the early 1930's, the trapping patterns and customs which had existed for generations began to change. Several families still used the land in the traditional way, staying out in the bush for the winter. Families surnamed Paul, Tebiscone, Costain, Pien-ose, Petremont, and others still trapped in groups on their traditional grounds. Other people of mixed blood built houses in Hunter's Point, growing gardens and clearing land for hay, and so created a mixed economy. Although men could now take on jobs elsewhere if they chose, the

Archie Perrier's store and trading post. The only person identified in this picture is Joe Decontie, the big man with the suspenders.

main income still came from fur. Similar changes had come about in other villages of the Kipawa region, especially in Brennan and Wolf Lakes.

By this time the Hudson's Bay Company no longer operated in the Kipawa region. Their nearest post was at Grand Lake Victoria. Fort Temiskaming had served the area from the time of its establishment by the French in 1682. The North West Company took control of the fort after the conquest of 1760; later the Hudson's Bay Company assumed control. There was another fort near the foot of the lake at Opimika, which was operated by one James Hunter, "the Orkneyman." (The Hudson's Bay Company recruited most of their post workers from the Orkney Islands, near Scotland.) James Hunter, father of Old Jimmie Hunter mentioned earlier, moved from Opimika to Lake Kipawa in 1847 and built another post called Hunter's Lodge, located near what is now known as Hunter's Lake. The post operated until 1902, at which time Fort Temiskaming and Opimika also closed, leaving the area open to independent traders and lumbermen. Competition had begun for the Hudson's Bay Company when the lumbermen, who also bought furs, reached Lake Temiskaming in 1836.

Hunter's Lodge, Hudson's Bay Post on Hunter's Lake.

In the 1920's and 1930's the missionaries scheduled summer visits; one in June and one in August. The June missionary visit was timed immediately after the trapping families arrival at Hunter's Point, Wolf Lake, and Brennan Lake. There were no scenes like those of the summer villages before the turn of the century. No muskets were fired; no headdresses were displayed. Even the drums were silent. Tradition had vanished; so had the spirit of congeniality that had marked other days.

Not all festivities had disappeared. There were still canoe races on the lake in front of the Catholic Church. Carrying contests and foot races continued on Archie's field, but they all lacked the color and verve of older times. The people of the bush were shy amid the glitter and pomposity of the church and the newly-found sophistication of their village cousins. Most of them wanted only to sell their furs and to return to their homes in the bush.

Even in the villages in those days, life revolved around the fur trade. For many the way of life had evolved from a total existence in the bush to one where people were able to grow food crops

A family hunting cabin of other years. In this picture, taken in the 1930's, it was being used by a party of American moose hunters.

sufficient for their own needs; meat and fish still came from the bush. But now a new problem emerged. Since these were depression years, strangers began to encroach on Kipawa territory from all directions. Fur-bearing animals were now getting scarce, resulting in many boundary disputes between the traditional family groups and the strangers.

This problem was foreseen as early as 1920. In that year, Chief Joe Petremont of Wolf Lake, together with Michel Shene and Jim Stanger of Hunter's Point, began action that they hoped would reserve the grounds for the exclusive use of the hunting families. They intended to create a hunting reserve for the registered "Indians" of the Kipawa region. It was seen as a way to protect the livelihood of the Natives who gathered their life's sustenance directly from the land, but they had also hoped to make a provision for the Métis (half-breeds). Shene's idea at the time was simply to reserve the land as it had been traditionally divided among family groups. In other words he sought government recognition of the Native people's rights and title for the land, in the same manner as the same government recognized those rights for itself and other members of society. He had heard that farmers, lumbermen, and even priests had pieces of paper proving their land ownership, and so he felt that for the people who had always lived here there was no question of their right.

Petremont, Shene, and Stanger visited all families to discuss with them a petition and a plan to set up a reserve. They believed that if they convinced most of their people to accept the plan and prove the fact with the names on a petition, the government in Ottawa would hear their plea. The majority approved the plan; Petremont, Shene, and Stanger went to Ottawa to represent their people's wishes.

Shene, it is said, had looked forward to his trip to Ottawa. As he explained to his people, he himself had been told that the site of the Government of Canada was close to where the Rideau River flows into the Ottawa. This had been the site of one of his family's camps when he was a boy. His family had been forced to leave the Rideau River when men bearing pieces of paper called "titles" confronted them with orders that they would have to move. Explaining that these titles were very powerful pieces of paper because they carried the government's word, they added that the government had given their land to other people who were going to use it for better purposes. The Shenes were told that they should move upstream where there was plenty of land.

Shene's family moved several times, each time finding that they had encroached on another family's territory. Now he was disturbed; the same thing that had happened years before on the Rideau was now happening here in Kipawa. Since 1900 strangers from the south—lumbermen, farmers, trappers, to mention only a few—were popping up here and there throughout the territory claiming land with these pieces of paper from the government. He felt that the wise thing to do was to obtain a similar piece of paper, a land title, for each family.

Now that the railway had reached South Temiskaming, the trip to Ottawa was not the arduous undertaking it had been in the old days. Making the trip cost money, and so did the clothing that would befit the representatives of the people. Money was hard to come by. A collection was taken up to finance the trip; even then, clothing for the trip was borrowed. With last-minute consultations, the three envoys were given an optimistic send-off on their way to the seat of government.

They paddled from Hunter's Point, through Turtle Narrows, and across Lake Kipawa to Gordon Creek, then went on to the village of Temiscaming. For the first time in their lives, Shene and Petremont boarded a train; how different this must have been from the old way of paddling for weeks to reach Ottawa. All this was old hat to Jim Stanger.

When they got to Ottawa, Shene found that it bore little resemblance to his childhood image. Ottawa was now a sprawling city even by southern standards; imagine what it must have looked like to bushmen. Neither Shene nor Petremont spoke much English. Since Jim Stanger had a reasonably good command of the language, he acted as interpreter. Shene, it seemed, understood government as being an individual, for he insisted on seeing the government at his house ("where he lives—the government.") He must have been taken aback when he came to the House of Commons to find dozens of people arguing over the affairs of the country.

According to Stanger, they eventually got shunted over to the Department of Indian Affairs, where they faced ridicule from its bureaucrats. They spared no punches. They wanted to know how "you Indians" could afford the train fare to Ottawa, how they had paid for their fine clothes, and why they had come to Ottawa when they could have gone to the agent.

Shene especially seemed to have been singled out for abuse, of which he understood very little. From Stanger's account, he mentioned that the Parliament Buildings were located on his family hunting grounds, apparently annoying some of the bureaucrats by saying this. (A small allowance he had been receiving from the government for an unknown reason, possibly as compensation for the land his family had surrendered, was cancelled when he returned to Hunter's Point.) Nevertheless, Shene persisted, repeating his family's experience of losing their land on the Rideau through the presentation of the papers from the government. Because he feared the same event could happen again on the Kipawa, he asked that papers be made up to protect the rights of his people out in the bush. Since government protected their own people with paper titles, it also had the power to protect *his* people.

The bureaucrats behaved as though Shene's ideas were preposterous. Through the interpreter they chided Shene, asking,

"What do you know about laws, old man?" Shene replied that the land was being spoiled by outsiders and that if this continued his people would someday have nowhere to trap or hunt. The bureaucrats remained adamant. They insisted that the Indian Agent knew everything there was to know about the land and the problems, and his friends and he should return to Kipawa to deal with him.

The three leaders were further advised that the government knew how much land there was and how much was needed by each family. The government would not register land for their people because there was more than enough to go around. Besides, what did they know about the laws that govern such things? The final bit of advice from the bureaucrats was that if their land was being encroached upon by outsiders, they would have to make better use of smaller hunting grounds.

Needless to say, Shene was unhappy by the racism those officials had displayed. Having been led to believe by the clergy and minor officials that the government was equally just to all people, he was shocked to learn how wrong they had been. If government were truly just, why would they not protect the rights of the hunting families?

To Shene the message from government was clear, but he could not reply in English. Government felt no obligation to protect the rights of the Native people and it was doubly demoralizing for him to return with that message. Previously he thought that to be on the side of government meant something. Informing him of the Indian Act, the Indian Agent had stressed how government made it their duty to look after his people through that piece of paper. Could it be possible that the Indian Act was designed to put him and his people down? From his own experience he had learned that any time Indians in the Kipawa had been helped by the Indian Agent, it was only after he had ensured others that the action would not interfere with any commercial enterprise in the territory.

When he returned to Hunter's Point with the message that they had failed, Shene announced that he would have no more to do with the government. Saying that the government was crooked, he stressed that the pieces of paper sanctimoniously passed around were nothing more than lies. In his opinion, government was only a tool for evil men and that the Indian Act was something different from what the people had been led to believe.

Nevertheless, the government did pay heed to similar complaints from the Natives located northeast from Kipawa territory. Clashes between outside trappers and the Indians had developed, some of them turning into gunfights resulting in the killing of two persons. Encroachment by poachers, with the tacit approval of government, had touched off that explosion. As in Kipawa, the intention of the poacher had been to sneak into the territory to kill as much game as he possibly could, then move on to other areas. Fotunately, the word of the priests of the Oblate Order made on behalf of the Natives made an impact on government, and the problem received some recognition.

In 1928, by an Order in Council, a Reserve was established to protect the hunting and trapping rights of the Grand Lake Indians. The reserve took in an area of approximately eight thousand square miles, including a part of the Kipawa territory, and so the families that lived there gained some protection. However, most of the remaining area comprising Kipawa still received no protection whatsoever from government.

If one had been on the shores of Lake Kipawa in the summer of 1902, one would have seen this Hudson's Bay Company birchbark canoe and others, as they transported bundles of furs and birchbark out to the Ottawa River. *(Charles Macnamara Collection, Ontario Archives)*

Kipawa, 1979. In 1979 the traffic on the lake is generally high-powered boats and airplanes. A highway now serves this shoreline. The tranquility of this scene gives little indication of the turmoil in the hearts of the shoreline dwellers whose homes are under threat.

The callous handling of the Kipawa representatives by the Department of Indian Affairs led to a hardening of attitudes among the people in the territory. Since there was no protection, the traditional conservation methods were given up. Most trappers and hunters felt that if they left breeders for restocking they would only invite the poachers. From a system of conservation that had sustained a good animal supply for countless generations, game management in Kipawa degenerated into a free-for-all. Today in Kipawa, a government system called the Licensed Trapping Grounds has exacerbated that situation.

CHAPTER SEVEN

Agriculture and its Social Effects

At the turn of the century, life changed from a hunting society to one of permanent villages sustained by gardens and hay farms. Hunter's Point, Wolf Lake, and Brennan Lake became villages, all with stores, churches, and schools. This chapter relates mostly to Hunter's Point, the larger of the three villages, which had 150 people in the 1930's. Old Paugene, it seems, led the way with his little farm above Depotie Lake. Although the mixture of the two races and cultures contributed to this change, the decisive reason was the operations that the lumber companies had begun. These companies brought in workers and horses, immediately creating a demand for vegetables and hay which the Natives supplied. So, the Native economic base shifted from hunting to agriculture and lumbering.

Hay fields of Hunter's Point.
(Courtesy of Doris Hansen)

Generally, families of mixed blood began these little settlements. Founding Wolf Lake were families bearing the names of Robinson, Young, Laroque, and Lavigne. Hunter's Point was founded by other families: Perrier, Hunter, Hansen, Moore, Boudrias, McLaughlin, Lariviere, and McDonald. Brennan Lake was started by the Robinsons and the LaFrances. Many of the registered "Indians" remained living in the bush on their ancestral grounds as they always had, but they came to visit and spend their summers at these new villages. For the people of the bush, the new villages were a mixed blessing. There were more store goods and home comforts in

Women worked indoors and out at harvest time. Irene Perrier (Simon) has this find old horse under control.

the village than in the summer camps in the bush, but they missed the tranquility of the forests. At least another generation would pass before the registered "Indians" also became villagers.

One would have expected a dull life in the villages: although there were radios, few families could afford one. There was no such thing as television. But life was anything but dull and the activities were many. Everyone did a lot of physical work, keeping themselves fit and trim. Rarely did people suffer from nervous breakdown, high blood pressure, or heart problems. In the winter months, most of the men attended to the traplines; they were located anywhere from twenty to one hundred miles from home. Those located closer to home came in frequently, while those who were farthest away might get home only for Christmas and Easter. When the father was out on the trapline, there was plenty to do at home. Usually the mother had several children to love, clothe, and feed. The mother made most of the clothes for children from hand-me-downs or yard material. All food was natural then, requiring a good deal more cleaning and preparation than today's instant wonders.

A boy or two growing up had numerous chores: watering and feeding the livestock, cleaning the stable, splitting and hauling wood, and shoveling snow.

But life for a woman without a mate was hard. This was true of Agnes Hayman.

Agnes's first marriage was to Dave St. Denis and they had ten children, when Dave became unable to trap for reasons of health. Agnes took to the trapline to make a living for her young family. When her oldest son Notoway (Isadore) reached fifteen, he and his younger brother Paddy, fourteen, took over the responsibility of supporting the family. Notoway died from a very tragic accident in his first winter of trapping. While hunting partridge in early March, he was snowshoeing over crusted snow when he broke through the crust. The gun discharged in the scramble and blasted one of his legs. He died almost immediately.

Agnes had to once again return to the trap grounds with Paddy to ensure her family's livelihood. It was during this time in 1943 that we broke trail for each other to get to our winter hunting grounds which were in close proximity. During the time that her family was growing up, Agnes was mother and provider to her remaining eight

Agnes Hayman, setting out for the winter's trapping and hunting. *(Courtesy Agnes Hayman)*

children. And even after her family has grown up, she continues to trap for a living. Today in her seventies, Agnes's main preoccupation is still trapping, hunting, and fishing.

The time for the big emotional release of the year was Christmas. If the men home from the bush had had a good hunt, they could pay off the store keeper and still have a few dollars left to buy gifts for the family and perhaps squander for their own pleasures. Preparing for Christmas amounted to an ordeal for the mother of the family. She baked and cooked over a hot stove for days in advance; she sewed, patched, and washed endless piles of clothing for the big festive season. On top of all that, there was always the possibility that the Christmas parcel from Eaton's or Simpson's would not arrive on time; meaning that Santa would be late in arriving. In winter or summer, mail was delivered every second week, contributing in one way to the state of sobriety in the village. In those days, anyone living in semi-isolated locations could obtain whiskey legally only by writing the Quebec Liquor Commission in Quebec City. Each order

Doris Perrier standing before the winter's supply of stove wood. *(Courtesy Doris Hansen)*

was restricted to one bottle, and delivery took four weeks. Anyone inclined to overindulge had a month to get it out of his system before ordering more.

The highlight of the Christmas holiday was the school concert. Several evenings during the month or more before Christmas, the school teacher held rehearsals for the children playing in the Yule performance. By far the most popular performances were those skits featuring little girls, dolls, and Christmas carols. There was also a place for the more serious plays with adults: a talent show where people of all ages played the fiddle, told jokes, strummed a guitar, and sang their rendition of a song popular of the time. It was family entertainment with very little external stimulation. Parents pulled their small children to the concert on sleighs; if everybody had brought their dogs, there would be more noise outside the hall than inside. All the kids had a chance to perform before their parents, and the happiness of the occasion created many pleasant memories.

After the Christmas concert was over and the children were safely home, a dance was held. There were several kinds: square-dances, round-dances, and step-dances. The musicians played the fiddle, guitar, accordian, piano, or organ; and just about everyone played one instrument or another. One of the traditions of the past was the Indian drum. Tenise Langevin (sometimes known as Pap-ig-osh) was the last musician to use the traditional Indian drum in Hunter's Point; he was the great grandfather of the Samuel and Mongrain families of Kipawa. At Christmas and other special occasions he performed some of the traditional rituals. He also adapted his drumming to accompany the violin.

By the tenth of January, most of the trappers returned to their grounds. The social whirl over, life in the village returned to normal. Because the hunting territories became crowded, several men were taking other jobs. Seasonal work was available in surveying, dam construction, mining exploration, lumbering, and timber cruising.[20] A man often hired himself out with his dog team in that enterprise or to deliver mail and supplies to post offices, trading posts, and winter camps.

Sports in the winter could not be well organized since most of the men were absent most of the time. However, a lucky development took place in the early 1930's when some Norwegians introduced skiing in the region. The young people of Hunter's Point began to make their own skis. We did not make skis to travel cross-country as the Norwegians did; we made them for down-hill ski runs and jumps. The skis were roughly hewn by axe, planed with a block plane and finished off according to the individual's workmanship and artistic desire. They were made from maple or yellow or white birch. The skis were attached with nothing more than a leather toe-strap into which the skier kicked his toe. A trail was cut through the trees on one of the largest hills of Hunter's Point and a good jump was created at the bottom to add to the thrill of the run. One of the hazards of the ski jump was the single-toe strap. Occasionally, a jumper might find himself hurtling through space with only one ski or none at all.

People assembled at the ski hill every night of the week and skied or jumped, oblivious of the weather or the darkness of the night. There was also a toboggan run on one side of the hill. Eight and

---

20. Timber cruising was a way of estimating timber stands by walking and recording samples at intervals on a grid system. Today, much of the information is obtained from aerial photographs.

ten-foot toboggans were in common use then for they replaced sleighs with dog teams. They could be borrowed on the promise to avoid trees. Sundays would find almost everybody who could walk at the ski hill. Those who did not ski or toboggan enjoyed watching the speed of the competitors, the distance of a jump, and the length of the slide out on to the lake ice.

Hockey never did catch on, mostly because a rink could not be supported by so small a group. By the mid 1930's, however, NHL hockey was broadcast over the radio, creating avid interest among some members of the community in the game, enough for the boys to play a shinny game at school on slush ice with homemade sticks and tin-can pucks.

Generally speaking, the school-age boys carried on as most healthy, rambunctious boys do everywhere else—ending up with torn clothing and bloody noses from fist-fighting and wrestling. Their ambitions were not so much in line with formal education as in trapping, hunting, fishing, or working in the bush on some other job. For that reason, the village people gained a reputation as the best bushmen in the country but were weak academically. On the other hand, the girls were better behaved and performed better as students. They learned quickly that creating pleasant surroundings at home led to social and romantic approval. So from their mothers, they learned the skills and benefits of being a good wife and a loving mother through cooking, sewing, and housekeeping. The pride of a family could be seen in the cleanliness of the home, the garden, and their children's clothing, as well as the upkeep of their equipment and animals. The focus of life in those days was the family. By today's standards we would have been judged impoverished; nevertheless, we had pride, independence, and a decent life.

It might be expected that life slowed down in the dead of winter, but that was not so. There was school every day for the young and as a rule they couldn't wait to get out of the schoolhouse and up to the ski hill. The older men fished through the ice with nets and baited lines, while the older women were usually hard at work making mitts, moccasins, socks, and snowshoes. The mothers of the village were generally busy feeding and clothing their families but still finding time to gossip. Mail delivery every two weeks invariably brought in news that travelled the village network from door to door.

A wedding reception for Louis Mathias and his bride Florence at Jones's home in Hunter's Point, 1936. *(Courtesy Hanna Reynolds)*

When there was time to listen to stories, there was always Louis the elderly craftsman working amid the pungent smell of smoked hides, who would fill his young visitors with the wonder of other days. As he spoke, the moose and deer hides that had been tanned in the summer now took the shapes of moccasins and mitts under his skillful hands. All the while, Old Louis would recall how, in his younger days, he paddled to James Bay as a Hudson's Bay voyager. Old Chizebeth (Mrs. Louis) used to catch two hundred rabbits in a good year, which became woven into one good double rabbit-skin blanket. She would first dry the skins by hanging them loosely in the frost, then cut them into strips. Sewn end to end, the strips were then woven in a criss-cross pattern, somewhat like basket weaving, to form a blanket.

While they worked, the old folks welcomed visits from the young. They felt that their function was a vital one; it was. Before the advent of synthetic clothing and snowmobiles, moose-hide moccasins and mitts were essential to winter travel in the bush. The knowledge that the elder craftsmen were anxious to pass on was not merely their art and craftsmanship but also the heritage of their own way of life and that of the generations that went before them. Unfortunately, much of the heritage and culture that they represented has been

Joe Meness with his wife Theresa (Wabi) and family. Counter-clockwise, the children are Theresa, Maxime, J.H., Beatrice, Margaret, and Mary. *(Courtesy Richard Meness)*

downgraded and lost to the present worship of material things. It is neither possible nor desirable to turn the clock back, but our Native ancestors must be remembered for their true place in the life and history of this land. As a youngster I was once treated to an individual view of life by Joe Meness, an elder and sage from Brennan Lake. He said:

> Our ancestors are the foundation for what we are today, both in body and spirit, as we will be the foundation for those who follow. They are the essence of our being and forever important. Those ancestors who preceeded us are buried in the land of Kipawa, and their spirits are immersed in the spirit of this land, as are those of the people yet unborn. All life and all things follow a cycle: the body dies but the spirit lives forever. It returns to the universal spirit, as do raindrops to a lake. Rabbits reach

the height of their cycle about every seven years when they become most plentiful. But without predators, the rabbits soon become too plentiful and nature soon causes a fall in the population by shortages of food or by sickness. Like the rabbit, the Nishnabi have a physical cycle. But in addition the Nishnabi have a cycle of spirit which finds its genius in the soil, the water, and the air of this land. This spirit will again revive the people in time.

When the Great Spirit moves to revive the true spirit of the Land of the Nishnabi, it will appear through the words of a few enlightened individuals. It will seem slow and sluggish at first but will gain momentum as more people learn the meaning of spiritual power. The Great Spirit gave birth to our ancestors of this land many, many thousands of years ago and bestowed His abundance of life-giving animals and vegetation as a sacred trust not to be destroyed wantonly. We should never forget this sacred trust, for to do so would be to betray our ancestors and the people yet unborn. The true spirit of life was once bountiful upon this land. It will be again, but first there will be destruction. When the Nishnabi is ready to fulfill his fate, it will be as a service to humanity and all living things.

In those times, forty or fifty years ago, when Joe Meness and others like him spoke of the wanton destruction of the trees, the animals, the fish, and the poisoning of the waters, few believed it could ever happen. The bush was vast and impenetrable and the waterways were hazardous to all except for the people who lived as part of the environment. They were as familiar with the country as a farmer is with his fields. People like Joe had no word for technology, but they somehow sensed impending destruction and waste. They did not speak under the shadow of doom or despair; their tales depicted an era of rebirth arising from an era of destruction. Often they captioned their word pictures with, "Whatever must happen in the meantime will happen."

The stories of the elders were not the only ones told. From time to time, different trappers would arrive to narrate their adventure with a pack of wolves or their long days spent tracking a fisher. There was always an audience of eager young aspiring trappers, their ears cocked to every word, anxious to learn each technique and trick of the trade. The guys who returned from mapping surveys to near and far places also had their yarns to tell about strange, faraway places and even stranger personalities.

During the week before Easter the men returned home from whatever kind of work they might have been doing in the bush or abroad. Everyone was ready for a party. Since most villagers observed lent, the party was postponed until after Easter. Then a real shindig would break out; a square-dance might be combined with a box social and a euchre (card-playing) party and perhaps even a talent or a lying contest.

The box social was a popular way of raising money and no wonder! The social involved lunch boxes decorated and filled with the most delicious food by the women. These boxes were displayed and opened to bidding by the men. The highest bidder for each box not only got a good meal, but he could also dine with the lady who had prepared the lunch. The monies collected this way went to the church or school.

The talent contests were always fun. It is really quite amazing how much entertainment can originate from 150 people. It always seemed, however, that the least talented made the most noise, a universal quality that has its counterparts at all levels of society.

The contest for the biggest lie—who could forget that? The stories were great because of their humor and local flavor. I had the good fortune of attending the last lying contest held in Hunter's Point when I was about nine years old. The prize winner was told by Jim McLaughlin. Jim was widely known for his fantastic stories and wonderful good humor—this was how his last story went:

> I was fire-ranging on Ross Lake at the time this happened, myself and Austin Adams. We had been brushing a couple of portages on the route to Ogascanan and were returning across Ross Lake when a sudden storm came up. Before it hit, there was a deafening noise from the wind and rain that seemed to be cork-screwing towards us. Austin was screaming at the top of his voice. I yelled back at him to sit flat in our birchbark

Corbeau Rock, the site of Jim McLaughlin's fabled landing. At the time this picture was taken it was known by its Nishnabi name "Kagagiwabik," which means the same as *Corbeau* in French or Raven in English. *(Archives of Ontario)*

> canoe and grip the gunwales. When that cork-screw hit us we couldn't see a thing, just a sensation of floating and being buffeted about like in a rapid. We swirled and swayed for what seemed like eternity... Then as suddenly as it started, we were down on the water again in little clouds of mist, which were the only evidence left by the storm. We looked around. Lo and behold! Corbeau Rock on Lake Kipawa... Believe it or not, we had flown our little birchbark canoe thirty miles from Ross Lake to Kipawa!

Another story that Jim liked to tell was about a horse named Sam who went wild:

> It was while I was in charge of the lumber depot at Ross Lake that one of my horses started to give me trouble.

This damned horse didn't like the harness or anything else that looked like work. Finally one day in the fall, he just wandered off into the bush and didn't return. I kept getting reports from Old Mathias during the winter about this horse that was yarding with the moose—a horse with a long, shaggy mane and a habit of browsing in the hardwoods. Old Mathias suggested shooting him, but I said, "No, don't shoot him; Sam'll come back." I didn't hear any more until the spring when another trapper said that he had seen a wild horse on the Kipawa River. I went down there the next day to bring my horse home. Sure enough, just as the trapper had said, there was Sam wading up the Kipawa River with a big pike in his mouth. I realized right there that Sam wasn't meant to be a farm animal. A horse who had learned to browse with the moose and fish like an otter had no business pulling a plough.

The spring hunt began shortly after Easter and usually finished about two weeks after the ice had disappeared from the lakes. Trappers came in from all directions with bundles of fur. The centre of life then became the two stores where new clothes were purchased, soft drinks were bought, and the trappers swapped tales about the hunt.

The Catholic Missionary arrived each spring a couple of weeks after the last trapping group had come in from their grounds. Father Martel was the priest of my time. He is still alive and well at ninety-four, living in an Oblates' home in Ste. Agathe, Quebec.

The Catholic mission lasted for about a week. In the early morning about seven o'clock, you would see canoes converging on the church from all directions. The priest would say Mass, which took nearly an hour, then he would open up the vestry where he had all kinds of prayer beads, medals, holy cards, holy water, and trinkets for sale. Father Martel was quite an accomplished photographer. He would take pictures one year and bring them back the following year as postcards for sale. The mission was a big event in the lives of most people, for they believed strongly in the religion, or at least feared it strongly. In any event, neither wind nor rain could stop the canoes loaded with families who paddled to Mass in the morning or Vespers in the evening. When his mission was

Arch Perrier Jr. and his wife Laura (Boudrias) and children. Laura was the first to graduate from grade school in Hunter's Point. This picture shows the family going to church. The canoe was the most versatile vehicle of the time and this typifies how it was used in everyday life.
(Courtesy Doris Hansen)

finished at Hunter's Point, the priest would go on to Wolf Lake and Brennan Lake to minister to the rest of his flock. The route to Wolf and Brennan Lakes has some treacherous rapids and long portages which required the skills of a capable canoeman. Frank Robinson carried out this function for a number of years.

There was also a Presbyterian congregation in Hunter's Point. Their church was a handsome little square-timber building in the trees opposite Archie's store. A student minister regularly spent the summer serving the small congregation.

The first school was opened in 1918 at Hunter's Point under the

Mrs. Lemieux (Ke-so-quay), Mrs. Robinson (Juliette Wabiko) and Mr. and Mrs. Ti-Louis England relaxing on the steps of the Catholic Church after the service. *(Courtesy Hanna Reynolds)*

Brennan Lake at mission time in the 1930's. *(Courtesy Hanna Reynolds)*

Frank Robinson and Raymond Richer in one of the rapids on the Kipawa River. This picture was taken on one of the annual trips with Father Martel, the Catholic missionary. *(Courtesy Wallace Moore)*

The Presbyterian Church, Hunter's Point. *(Courtesy Doris Hansen)*

This log building was the first school in Hunter's Point; it was operated under the auspices of the Presbyterian Church. This picture was taken in 1914. *(Courtesy Doris Hansen)*

sponsorship of the Presbyterian Church. It was located at the east shore of the lake south of Archie's store. Two years later another school was opened by the Department of Indian Affairs and operated by the Catholic Church. That school was a single room where classes from grades one to eight were held; only one teacher carried the load. Believe it or not, it had central heating—provided by a big pot-bellied stove that sat in the centre of the room. The boys brought in wood as it was needed. To discipline thirty to forty children in all grades inside a single room the teacher had to be tough. She was a resourceful person on that score. On occasion she had to bring out the pointer or the strap to quell a minor rebellion that broke out once in a while. In the seven years that I went to school I had two teachers, Annie Marcotte and Christina Nephin. Both of them were dedicated. Every fall at freeze-up time, if the students had been behaving reasonably well, the teacher would declare a holiday or two. This came about because when the lakes froze over, snow usually followed within a day or two. Those were the only days we had to skate during the year; there were no ploughs with which to clear the snow from the lake.

The first person to graduate from the Indian Day School was Laura Boudrias, who passed her entrance exam in 1930. Afterwards, one

School House—Brennan Lake. *(Courtesy Doris Joly)*

or two pupils graduated from the school every year until it closed in 1968. Unfortunately, there was no opportunity for any of the graduates of grade school to continue their education. The nearest high school was located in Temiscaming, and the cost of boarding anyone away from home was beyond the means of most families.

The school house, being the only public building other than the two churches, served as the social centre for the community.

Summertime activities were many and varied. The people of the village were now planting, cultivating, and harvesting crops. Their other activities included playing ball, fishing, hunting, guiding, fire-ranging, and others.

Planting was everybody's business. Everyone used ploughs pulled by horses, except Hans Hansen who used a team of oxen. If a family did not have a horse it would borrow one from a neighbor and plow up the land. When that was done, all members of the family who could lift a hoe or rake were obliged to do their share of back-breaking work until the crop was planted. That was not the end of the work by any means. All summer long the rows and beds had to be hoed, weeded, and watered—and water had to be hauled by the bucket from the lake or stream.

A baseball field was hacked out of the bush on the hill behind Jones's. Hunter's Point was too small to form a team of any particular age group, so it was not unusual to see an eight-year-old

Hans Hansen's team of oxen were reduced to one ox and one horse by the time this picture was taken in 1924. *(Courtesy Doris Hansen)*

hopeful follow a white-thatched sixty-year-old to the plate. It was community recreation rather than competition. By far the biggest thrill I can remember of those games was the time we beat every team of Americans that passed through Hunter's Point one summer. When I say "team" I don't mean that they were professional baseball teams; they were canoeists. There were several camps in the Temagami area for college students. Canoeing was taught at those camps, and their boys went on wilderness canoe trips, some going as far as James Bay. Fortunately for us, Hunter's Point was on their route, and the boys usually laid up for three or four days. They travelled in groups of ten to twelve canoes, two boys to every canoe, and the parties were spaced out about a week apart. The first summer we played them we lost every game, but we won them all the next summer. Possibly the best player ever produced in Hunter's Point was Jimmie Hunter, the son of Pete and Flora Hunter. He later lost his life in Italy before his nineteenth birthday fighting in World War II.

Fish was our staple diet during the summer. We did not fish for sport—although it was always enjoyable—we fished because we lived by it. The killing of moose and deer in the summer was for the same reason. When there was a need for meat in the summer one of the hunters would go out and kill a moose and bring it in by

A birchbark canoe made by Phillip Hayman, probably the last one made in Hunter's Point. The paddler is Doris Perrier. Note the side-wheeler towboat on the right, the C.J. Booth by name. *(Courtesy Doris Hansen)*

canoe. It was customary then to share the meat amongst the families that needed it. In those days without refrigeration, no meat was wasted or spoiled. Every part of the moose was used except the hoofs and the bones.

Guiding for tourist fishermen was a popular occupation in the Temagami Lake region in the 1920's and 1930's and a good number of men from Kipawa went there to guide. Kipawa, however, was better known for its moose hunting.

Because of the depression, it was very important to have tourists. For some men, guiding was the only source of income between the spring hunt and the fall. Maps, if there were any at all, were inaccurate. The only mode of travel was by canoe. There were no highways; only portage and water routes. Small wonder that everyone outside the territory hired guides, even the surveyors there to make maps of the area.

Hunters, mostly Americans, came in by rail to Kipawa, then boarded Robbie Cunningham's passenger and freight boat to sail for Turtle Portage. Here they were met by Roy Jones for the final lap to Hunter's Point. From there the trip and the hunt were all by canoe. The tourist hunter was invariably taken to the hunting grounds of the guide where a cabin awaited them. The guide knew approximately how many moose there were and where they would be found. Cows

A birchbark canoe nearing completion by Bob Mongrain in 1944. *(Courtesy Violet Mongrain)*

and calves were never shot and the guides were extremely careful that moose would not be wounded by a shot from too great a distance. Proper conservation to the guide affected the food sources of his family, so the matter was never far from his mind.

Berry picking was one of those activities that figured prominently in the preservation of food for winter. It was a family endeavor that gave the young people a lot of pleasure. It was not unusual to see an eighteen-foot canoe carrying ten to twelve persons across the lake to Archie Perrier's farm, where wild strawberries growing in profusion awaited them. Later in the summer, all the mountains that had been burnt over were loaded with blueberries. The blueberry crop is one that grows in the wake of forest fires, generally two years after the fire. It is said that giant-pine forests produce the best blueberries, but what a price to pay for blueberries! Blueberry picking excursions were a regular affair. The most enjoyable were those to Ostoboning Lake. A great part of the heavy pine forests of Ostoboning had been burnt by a disasterous fire in the late 1920's. The ashes were so thick that several years had passed before trees began to grow again. Millions of feet of virgin timber had gone up in smoke, as well as much precious animal life. Old Mr. Jones, a long time resident of Hunter's Point, said that the blueberry crop was so rich a few years after the fire that when attempting to climb the hilly portages around Ostoboning, he could make no headway for slipping back on the blueberries crushed under his feet.

The daily family excursion to islands of Ostoboning during the blueberry season began early in the morning with a great din of children's voices and barking dogs; they always seemed to go together. Preparation for the trip began with packing a lunch that was more than likely fortified by loaves of fresh bread and butter. We always brought along fishing gear, which, in those days, consisted of a thick green line with hooks for stillfishing and a spinner for trolling. With the hook and line and a frog for bait we seldom failed to get fish for lunch. Our little flotilla of four or five canoes would set out loaded to the gunwales, paddled by the adults of each family. There was no getting away from the dogs. They dashed along the shores and swam the narrows trying to keep up. Thrilled by the performance of the dogs, the kids cheered them on with shouts and whistles.

I have tried in this chapter to review briefly how life changed from a purely trapping and hunting society to several agricultural and lumbering settlements. In doing this, I touched on the various factors of change commencing with the first attemps of growing crops of vegetables and hay. The people of mixed blood, given their varied background, contributed to the opening and development of these communities. An economy based in part on agriculture allowed for a more permanent community where wage employment was also available. The new economy also changed the social practices to some degree and allowed for various kinds of recreation and entertainment that was impossible in the summer villages. I brought into the picture a way of life that adapted to the necessity for the men to be absent for much of the time. The feasts of Christmas, Easter, and other occasions were possible thanks to participation of everyone in the community. Schools, churches, and other institutions, whether good or bad, were brought in. Even berry picking played important and economic functions in the village. As money became more readily available in the wage economy, however, and the fur resources dwindled, people were obliged to move out.

A valuable bovine inhabitant of Hunter's Point. *(Courtesy of Doris Hansen)*

The people who moved to Kipawa had no previous experience with land title. The only time anything had been said about land titles previously was the attempt by Shene, Petremont, and Stanger to obtain title for the family hunting grounds in Kipawa; and that attempt had been ridiculed by the bureaucrats in Ottawa. Ownership to cleared land in the villages had been subject to natural law for centuries previous. If a person cleared a strip of land, it was his. To even question his rights was unthinkable. To have mentioned land title to any of the villagers would have drawn blank stares. You owned land by clearing it. The villagers neither thought nor accepted that the land they had cleared and built on could belong to anyone else. For the people of the bush, land was something you earned by your work and sweat and had nothing to do with titles and licenses.

CHAPTER EIGHT

Lumbering

The advent of lumbering signalled the beginnings of the first real influence of colonial exploitation and expansion into the territory of Kipawa. The territory was covered with some of the finest white and red-pine stands in all of Canada. In the words of one elder who remembers it, "The hills and valleys were blue with pine for as far as the eye could see in all directions. It was like this everywhere on the Kipawa."

The technology of lumbering, of course, was important to the changes that came about in Kipawa, and so they will be briefly discussed here. So will their environmental impact. But no less important is the part that the Native people of Kipawa themselves played in lumbering. For this reason, the chapter is about them.

The first lumbermen who arrived around 1870 cut square timber. They operated until 1900. Their effect on the environment was minimal, and they took little timber. With nothing but an axe, saw, and tackle to their name, they could take only timber that stood near the shorelines of the lakes and rivers in the region. The lumbermen who were to follow had more equipment and so could harvest more.

Individual lumbermen had bought timber rights in Kipawa territory as early as 1866. By 1900 the lumber business had shifted from square timber to saw logs and, to satisfy a huge demand, lumber companies from the lower Ottawa River began buying up these timber limits. The saw-log operation employed far more men and equipment than the square-timber operators ever did, and logged off much larger areas.

Consequently, the damages to the environment reached much greater proportions. Logging roads, or main roads, ran to the choicest stands from the nearest lake or river. When logs were piled high on sleighs and drawn by horses, the road had to descend on a slope (called a draw) from its point of origin to its final destination at water level. Skidding trails (skidways), over which a man and horse skidded or dragged individual logs to log piles, ran from the timber operation to the main road. When the larger pine trees were felled, they smashed and broke the other trees in the vicinity. These trees were left amid the discarded pine tops. A tribute to man's dedication to money was reflected in the fact that logs accepted for saw logs had to be at least six inches at the top end. Thus, pine tops were left to rot in the bush. Other damaging effects came from the practice of taking only the choicest timber. Many trees found after felling to have slight defects were left to rot.

Lumber camp stables and log-hauling sleighs of the 1940's. *(Courtesy Gilbert Samuel)*

Another form of environmental damage came from the log drives. On the log-runs down the lakes and rivers, much of the bark from the logs worked loose and sank to the bottom. This was particularly so with logs that remained immersed in the water for more than a year. The results became most noticeable at the foot of rapids where layer upon layer of black rotting bark destroyed spawning beds for fish and ecosystems of other kinds. The lumber industry of other years created quite a few millionaires and left behind much devastation. The ecological damage was of no concern at the time because timber stands seemed endless, and steady wages became a strong incentive to work in the bush.

Still, the environmental damages of yesteryear were pristine compared to those caused by today's operations. In December of 1979, I drove to **Ostoboning Lake** over a newly-constructed logging

A log jam.   *(Courtesy of Charlie McKenzie)*

road, where an operation had just been completed. The site was one of total devastation, a graveyard of crushed and rotting trees that had not been profitable enough to remove. The disastrous fires of the 1920's were puny by comparison. At least, a fire in a coniferous forest will consume everything in its path, leaving the ground clear for reforestation. This operation crushed and destroyed everything in its path, leaving behind a tangled mass of broken trees that not only create barriers for men and animals alike, but also block any new growth. This tangled mass must rot away before any reforestation can begin. How long that might take—twenty, forty, or sixty years—is anybody's guess. Today, the Native people of Kipawa share none of the profits from their timber, not even as wage earners. The land is being denuded slowly for the profit of outsiders benefitting from the licenses granted them by the province of Quebec and the Government of Canada.

The first lumbermen to reach Lake Temiskaming were the McConnell brothers, who started an operation at the foot of the lake in 1836. A few of the people living in Kipawa trace part of their ancestry to the McConnell family. Oliver Latour, who put the first steamboat, *The Mattawa*, on Lake Temiskaming in 1882, was also the first to provide accomodation at Kipawa for lumbermen. He built a floating dock and shed off shore from the present site of Kipawa. His most lucrative provisions were fortified wines and

95

The Hurdman, a freight and passenger boat of a company by the same name. The Hurdman Company operated early in the century carrying freight and workmen for the lumber companies to the far-flung bays of Lake Kipawa. Old Quayse, a Native boatsman, was second in command for many years because of his knowledge of the passages, shoals, submerged rocks, and other hazards. In the days when there were inadequate maps and charts of the lake Native boatsmen captained many of the boats. *(Archives of Ontario)*

spirits, it is said, and he escaped the legal prohibition against serving liquor by floating.

Speculators were the first to learn of the timber limits (or berths as they were called then). The earliest available record of such a lease is of one George Bryson who took out a berth, shown as Gore No. 2, on the twenty-eighth of April, 1866, then later sold it to the Shepard Morse Lumber Company. Other individuals who bought and sold timber limits were Ben McConnell, James Man, J.N. Thompson, W.R. Thistle, J.P. Brennan, J. Ross, Thomas Glover, E.B. Eddy, D. Moore, E. Wright, W. Cobb, J.A. Grant, J. Francis, R. Ryan, E.E. Lauzon, W. Mohr, and John Roche. These limits were sold privately or at auction between 1900 and 1910 when the saw-log operation began in earnest and square-timber was no longer in demand. The larger companies which moved into the Kipawa territory were McLachlin Bros., Shepard Morse, the Hull Lumber Company, Hawkesbury, J.R. Booth, Molson's Bank, W.C. Edwards, Colonial Lumber Company, B. Grier, and Lumsden and Gillies Brothers Ltd.

One man with whom I was acquainted in my youth and who loved to recall memories of the early days of lumbering was Billy Jawbone. As a young man he had squared timber, lived in camboose camps (large shelters; see description below), and towed timber booms by cadge crib.

Billy had become competent with a broadaxe, a skill that was much in demand then, and spent a couple of winters squaring timber. He said that only the largest choice trees were taken and that they were hewn square to no less than twenty-four inches, at minimum lengths of forty feet. The likes of such trees do not exist anywhere in eastern Canada today. The finished timbers were hauled to the water's edge by teams of horses and floated.

The floating timbers were then gathered and chained in booms for towing. In those times, before the use of steam or gas-engine boats, the device used for timber towing was called a cadge crib; real horses provided the horsepower.

The cadge crib was a floating platform, about thirty feet square, with a primitive winch installed at its centre. The winch consisted of a wooden post that was securely fastened vertically through the timbers around which revolved a steel drum; this provided a wind-up mechanism. The towing power was created by two horses, harnessed to arms of the drum, walking in circles around the drum winding up the rope which pulled the cadge crib and the attached booms forward. Cadge cribbing was used in stretches of water where there was insufficient current to move the booms downstream.

The camboose camp he described was a large one-room log shanty which housed thirty to forty men in bunk beds that lined the wall. The room centre was occupied by an open fire place over which all the cooking was done; the smoke escaped through an opening in the roof. The walls were only high enough to allow a tall man to stand and the roof was covered with split logs called scoops. Beans, pork, beef, bread, and rice, accompanied by scalding tea in tin cups, was the total fare of the lumberjack, or shantyman, as he was sometimes called then.

Although by inclination Billy was a hunter and trapper, he soon acquired the skills of lumbering. He was an excellent log driver, though he couldn't swim. He was a top-loader, the fellow who stood on top of those high loads of logs and rammed each log into place. He captained a tow boat on Lake Kipawa, though he couldn't read or write. People, who worked with him on the boats, said that he had night vision like a cat and he knew the whereabouts of every submerged rock and shoal that dotted the log-towing channels.

Billy Jawbone.

Following the purchases of timber limits from individuals by the previously mentioned lumber companies, rapid changes began in many parts of Kipawa territory. Hay Bay was one of the first areas to feel the teeth of the cross-cut saw. It was just a matter of time before the lumber companies had cleared land and established farms and depots. Among them were Green's Farm on Lake Kipawa proper, Colonial Lumber at Sunnyside, Shepard Morse at Hunter's Point, David Moore Lumber on Ostoboning Lake (later to be bought by Hull Lumber), J.R. Booth at Sasaginaga, Grassy Lake, and Kipawa village, Klock's Lumber on Ross Lake, McLachlin at Red Pine, Brennan Lake, and Wolf Lake, and E.B. Eddy on Dumoine Lake. This list of lumber companies who operated on the Kipawa does not include all that operated there. Some companies flourished for a while in the service of hauling supplies and towing logs, then went out of business, leaving no records. Others worked for the larger companies as jobbers. In addition to these farms and depots there were several hay farms, stopovers, and half-ways enroute to the main sites. It was from those depots listed that the above lumber camps fanned out. Today they would be known as administrative and supply centres.

Since this is a history from a Native perspective I will leave the technicalities of the lumber operation at this point to indicate how Native people were involved. As I have been doing I choose the activities of one person to illustrate that involvement. In those times, any outsider having to travel the territory hired the people who had grown up there. This is why Antoine Endogwen[21] became a lumberman.

The eldest of four children, Antoine lived with his mother and three sisters in a little clearing near Ostoboning Lake, at the mouth of the Saseginaga and Cherry Rivers. His father had died when he and the other children were still young, obliging him to help his mother trap, hunt, fish, and garden. He became a trapper and hunter extraordinaire, a bushman in the best tradition. By the time he reached the age of sixteen, he was well known among his peers in the territory for these exceptional abilities. Hearing of Antoine's reputation as a bushman, the lumbermen of the area hired him to locate the best cuts of timber. He had a knack for choosing the best roadways for hauling the logs to the lakes or rivers where they would be floated.

American hunters from the states of New York, Pennsylvania,

---

21. Most of the information and accounts of Antoine Endogwen in this book were given by Gordon Moore, his half-brother who now lives in Kipawa.

Ohio, and Michigan came to know Antoine and vied for his services as guide and cheerful companion. It is said that, as a joke, he would carry two canoes at the same time over a portage.

Though a man of extravagant good humor, Antoine could also become angry. When the situation required him to do so, he could think and act quickly. He was excellence-in-motion as a physical specimen, standing six feet two inches and weighing 180 pounds. Highly intelligent, ingenious, he displayed an uncanny ability to hunt yet maintain rapport with his environment. His one apparent defect was that he was very hard of hearing. Men who hunted with him say that he seemed to have a sixth sense about animals, so overcoming his deafness.

Duncan Hunter once described to me how Antoine dealt with the problem of poachers. He said:

> We had paddled in from Ostoboning to B.L. Lake with enough supplies and trapping gear for the fall hunt. When he reached the lake, Antoine said, "I see smoke coming from my cabin; I wonder who's there." As we paddled closer a man stepped out of the door and Antoine recognized him as Menard—a well known poacher and sometime bully. As we approached, Menard showed every intention of taking over. I was fourteen then and a little scared that there was going to be a fight. When Antoine stepped out of the canoe he walked straight up to Menard, face to face at about two feet. You see, Antoine was very deaf and he wanted to hear Menard. He asked Menard what he was doing. Menard said he was there for the fall hunt. Antoine's only words were, "This is my ground." In a flash he seized Menard by the throat and hoisted him off his feet. There was no fight . . . Before Menard left Antoine boiled up a pail of tea and treated him to some fresh cookies, at the same time advising him where he might go to find someone who needed a hunting partner.

While in his teens Antoine became the assistant to Narcisse Morin, the Walker for the Hull Lumber Company. Today, Morin's position would be known as the Superintendent of Bush Operations. In late summer of each year Narcisse hired Antoine to help him survey the limit by canoe and on foot and plan the winter's logging operation. Antoine would sometimes work with him in winter when the log hauling started. He particularly liked the challenge of "top loading," which was the skill of stacking the logs as high as possible on the sleighs for hauling to the dump.

Archie Perrier and Antoine Endogwen repairing a canvas canoe. The building with the peak roof was the store and the one on the right was Archie's house, where he and his wife Rose raised ten children. Archie and Antoine had one very strong virtue in common; neither of them ever had a drink of alcoholic spirits. *(Courtesy Doris Hansen)*

Another job of note that he once did for a lumber company was that of moving livestock from a remote depot to the railway. When Klock's Lumber closed their depot on Ross Lake, they had several head of horses and cattle (perhaps forty or fifty) which had to be removed. They hired Antoine to move the livestock from Ross Lake to a railway terminal. Choosing to take them to Latullipe, located northwest of Kipawa, he hired Bob Mongrain and Barney Jawbone to help on this drive. They found that after they got away from the farm the animals followed very well. According to Bob Mongrain (the only partner of that trip still living), farm animals stick together instinctively when they travel in thick bush. In such an undertaking, the important thing was to choose a route through dense forests, lakes, and rivers that would get them there safely in the shortest time possible. In this respect Antoine was a master; he knew the territory in the way some people know their back yards. People used to say that he knew every lake, pond, mountain, and valley of each area that he trapped. As the crow flies, Ross Lake is thirty-five miles from Latullipe. Considering the round-about route they would have to take to avoid lakes and rivers too large to cross and mountainous terrain too rugged for the animals to travel, they probably travelled twice as far. They completed the journey, however, without losing a single animal.

Antoine travelled several times to the United States on invitation by well-to-do Americans. He went to the World's Fair in Chicago in 1933-34 and made several trips to West Virginia. On one of these trips he attended a state fair in Wheeling, where he was asked to participate by giving a demonstration in moose calling. In those days moose calling was an exotic art far removed from the plastic imitations we now know. He did his best moose imitation, but then his friends wanted even more. They decided to pull a little stunt to test Antoine's courage, skill, and ingenuity (perhaps even his sense of humor), by asking him to operate a dirigible, which was anchored at the fairgrounds. They made a deal with the pilot to allow Antoine to take the balloon up by himself, if he would agree to it. He agreed and so did the pilot, who briefed Antoine on the controls. Without any further hesitation Antoine took the balloon up, carried out a few manouevers, then brought it back to earth like a professional pilot.

Though Antoine figured prominently in the early stages of lumbering on the Kipawa, his natural inclinations were that of a trapper and hunter. He loved his Ostoboning home dearly. He lumbered, guided, fire-ranged, and even acted in a movie called *Silent Enemy*, that was made by the Burden Pictures Company in 1929. But, these were mere interruptions on a land that created his body and spirit over countless generations.

By 1910 the larger companies had completely taken over from the individual limit owner. These companies then created networks of depots and camps which usually followed a particular waterway for moving logs to market. The logistics of getting logs to the saw mill were essential to the success of logging, and direct towing was the easiest and least costly in getting the logs to the mill. Hay Bay had two advantages that the lumbermen looked for: one was the abundance of pine, which was characteristic on Kipawa, and the other was water deep enough to allow towing of logs. Much of the adventure and romance of the old days, however, originated with the river drives.

The Hull Lumber Company on Ostoboning operated many of their own camps, but also used contractors and jobbers to cut and float their logs to their Lumsden's mill at Temiscaming.

The C.J. Booth with a boom of logs bound for Gordon Creek. *(Courtesy Doris Hansen)*

J.R. Booth had depots at Kipawa village, Saseginaga and Grassy Lake, each supporting several lumber camps in their vicinity. The logs on the Saseginaga were driven down the river of the same name to Ostoboning and from there through Hunter's Point and across Lake Kipawa to Gordon Creek. They were then shipped down the Ottawa River to the mill near Hull.

McLachlin Brothers operated in similar fashion and had their depots at Red Pine, Brennan Lake, and Wolf Lake. They brought their logs down the mighty Kipawa River to Red Pine Chute where they floated into the peaceful waters of Lake Kipawa there to be towed for forty-eight miles to Gordon Creek and eventually down to the lower Ottawa River for sawing in Arnprior.

Barney Jawbone was one of the workers on the log runs. Many stories are remembered about Barney Jawbone. They might be stories of his prowess as a swimmer and diver, they may be about his uncanny ability to navigate through blinding fogs and pitch-black nights, or his natural instincts for hunting and fishing.

Everybody in Kipawa knows at least one story about Barney Jawbone so I am going to tell one that I experienced and one other that was told to me by George Mongrain more than thirty years ago.

When I was seventeen, I worked one summer as a fireman on the C.J. Booth. Barney was the Captain. We were anchored one evening along a sheltered shore waiting for the wind to change so we could continue towing our boom to Kipawa. Hooked on beside the C.J. was a scow which was partitioned in half to make a kitchen and sleeping quarters for the deck hands and boom men. Several of us were sitting around in the quarters playing cards and arguing, a short while after supper, when an anguished cry came from the kitchen. We rushed in to see what calamity had overtaken our favorite cook. He was standing on the deck gesturing towards the water. The elderly gentleman had somehow dropped his false teeth into the lake while he was throwing out the dishwater; now he was standing there cursing to high heaven for his misfortune. The sun was close to setting, which meant the light would soon be fading; already the shadows made it dark and murky.

One of the men went immediately to Barney's cabin to tell him of the mishap, knowing that Barney might be the only hope of retrieving the teeth. Dashing to the edge, he threw off his clothes and slipped into the water, then swam around to where the cook was standing. The cook pointed to the spot where his teeth had bitten the water. Barney floated around on the surface, acting for all the world like a beaver, peering at the bottom, adjusting his eyes to the dark shadows. He submerged with hardly a ripple and was soon lost in the depths. He broke surface again after what seemed like a perilously long period of time, but was likely less than two minutes. Without uttering a word he swam over to where the cook was standing on the deck and reached up with his closed hand, palm down. The cook cupped his hands and the missing teeth dropped

Monique and Barney Jawbone, and their two adopted children, Rudy and Marie.

into them. This act was indicative of Barney's silent, confident approach to life.

Years later Barney was warned by a doctor that he had a bad heart and that he would have to give up trapping. He ignored those orders and continued his robust way of life. He said that he would rather be dead than to sit around doing nothing. He died quietly one evening, in his seventy-fifth year, in his favorite chair watching TV, after a long day on the trapline.

George Mongrain, a boyhood chum and lifelong friend of Barney's, told of the time he and Barney went moose hunting. It was late in September and they were in on Clement Lake. It was one of those beautiful sunny evenings and they were waiting for the stillness that usually comes with sunset, before starting to hunt. They had pulled their canoe up near a huge beaver house and were just standing on the house, listening.

After a while Barney decided to take a swim. He told George of his intentions and silently faded into the bush along the shore. George said that he remained on the beaver house with his attention focused on the various sounds around, and had momentarily forgotten about Barney's leaving, when suddenly from underneath his feet came a booming voice, "Hey George!" It of course was Barney, but who would have expected a voice from inside a beaver house. George said that it startled him so that he lost his balance and darned near fell into the lake. Barney made some imitation beaver calls and gurgled around under a pile of feed directly in front of the house as he left it. He surfaced about twenty feet out, just like an old buck. This prank was typical of Barney when his personality was taken by a mischievous mood, which was quite often. He had walked out of sight along the shore, then swam back under water through the beaver passage and right into the house. That was Barney's practical joke for the day.

Native people worked in lumber operations until they shut down in the early 1930's. The work was mostly seasonal and could often be done during the off-season for trapping. Some saw it as an opportunity to give their trapping grounds a chance to replenish themselves. In any event they were fortunate to be able to return to their trapping when the lumber companies began to close down for the Great Depression had begun.

During those first thirty years of the century, Native people formed much of the work force for most of the companies. Knowing the land, they were hired for this knowledge. In addition they had the opportunity to work near home. They worked as foremen, loggers, skidders, filers, drivers, boatsmen, boom men, keepover men, cruisers, dam builders, teamsters, blacksmiths, and general handymen. Some of the men continued to operate the company farms after the companies had left.

The Native lumbermen set a high standard of workmanship in every area of lumbering, but they seemed to be especially adept at log driving, white water work (work in the rapids), and lake work. Perhaps this familiarity came from a thousand years of navigating these same waters with birchbark canoes. Frank Robinson, a half-breed from Wolf Lake, recounted an occasion which illustrates the hazards of white water (rapids) and the log drive.

> We were bringing down a good-sized boom for Booth. We had a gas boat, which I ran; so, they called me the gas-boat man. Gas boats were a new thing then; I think I was the first one to bring a boom down that river with a

Rapids on the Kipawa River. *(Archives of Ontario)*

gas boat, so I was learning what I could do with it. It was a big motor, twelve horsepower, big in those days back in 1918. It was set in the middle of a twenty-eight foot pointer. It had one cylinder and it shook like hell. Besides the gas boat, we had a winch boat (hand winch), and five pointer rowboats. Our drive crew consisted of a foreman, clerk, handyman, gas man, cook and a cook's helper, and about forty boatsmen. About three days before we were to reach Grand Calumet Chute, which was the most dangerous rapid on the Kipawa River, Alex, the foreman, began to complain of a sore wrist. The men were saying amongst themselves that he did this regularly to get out of running the worst rapids; and it seemed that it might be so, because the next morning he was wearing a strap on his wrist. He said that this was to ease the pain. As a rule the foreman, as bowsman, took the boats through the dangerous rapids. On our last day before Big Calumet, George Miller, the Walker (superintendent) showed up. If you don't know who George was, he was a big half-breed from North Temiskaming, who was as smart as a fox and strong as a bear, and he sure as hell liked white water. He guessed what was going through Alex's mind when he saw the leather strap, or maybe he was forewarned. Anyway he said to Alex, "I need a little fun Alex, do you mind if I take that goddamn gas boat through the Big Calumet?" Alex quickly agreed and his gloom lifted. As we prepared to run the boats through George said, "It's a good day for white water." The sky was clear and sunny about eleven o'clock in the morning. We snubbed the boom above the rapids so that we wouldn't have to contend with logs in the rapids and below. The gas boat was the first to go. George took the position as bowsman and with him a powerful young Gaspé fellow. I was at the motor and in the stern was another strapping good boatsman, a Notoway [Mohawk] lad. George stood high in the bow where he could read the currents and choose a passage to the first chute; there were two. One concern that I had was that we might scrape over a rock and take the propellor off. George waved to the point at which I was to take the rapid; this I did and cut her back to idle. I had been through quite a few rapids before, but this was the first time that I had to sit quiet with my hand on a throttle—it made me scared as hell. The water was high that spring and the swells we had to avoid at the centre were eight or ten feet high. George was avoiding that centre crest very well and I looked around to see how the sternsman was doing. He was okay, at least he was doing something, holding the stern tight so it wouldn't turn in the rapid. I had my eye on George as we hit the first dip. There was such a spray that I could hardly see those two guys up front. George was so high in the bow that he was damn near thrown into the white water. He backed up to better footing for the next one. The last drop was the worst one, the rapid narrowed and was quite steep and a lot of water funneled into a deep boiling hole on the right. If we were going to make it we had to

George Miller (left), pictured here with a Mr. Moore when he worked for Gatineau Power Co. George was a man of great physical power and endurance. *(Courtesy Abe Miller)*

avoid that hole. We went through the chute well enough, but then for a second or two we were heading for that hole. George yelled back at the sternsman to hold fast and he and his man up front pulled the bow over; at that moment, not knowing what else to do I gave her the gun, full steam ahead. The boat shot ahead and we got through with about six inches of water in the boat. George grinned when we hit shore and in his deep voice said, "You know Frank, if it wasn't for those twelve horses you have there, we might still be in that hole."

George Miller was a man of sound judgement who was able to adjust to different occupations as the need arose or as his natural curiosity demanded. He received no classroom education, but he did learn to read and write of his own volition. George's varied career and accomplishments point out the many capabilities he possessed. At thirteen years of age he was in charge of the first log drive through Gordon Creek; at twenty-one he was the youngest person to qualify for a lake captain's certificate. At one phase in his early twenties he hauled freight for the Hudson's Bay Company from Temiscaming to Grand Lake Victoria. He later became "Walker" for J.R. Booth. As Captain Miller he managed the Temiskaming Navigation Company for a number of years. At other times he captained boats on Lake Temiskaming, Kipawa and the Montreal River. After a career in lumbering he turned to employment in the hydroelectric field and became a master mechanic in charge of maintenance for the Gatineau Power Company in Temiscaming. This position he held for twenty-four years. George's wife and companion was the former Philomene Crawford, whom he married in 1903. She was from Mattawa; they had four children: Abe, Tony, Margaret, and Helena. Margaret, and Helena.

Among the local contractors who worked in the lumber business was Archie Perrier. Archie took on the job of driving and towing Booth's logs from Big Birch Lake, through Hunter's Point to Turtle Dam, a distance of about twenty miles. When he first began, it was with a gas boat and a couple of row boats, but then when McLachlin's operation on Brennan Lake began to slacken he rented their Alligator, the "Bonnechere," which has seen service with that company for many years on the lower Ottawa.

The Alligator, a steam-driven, wood-fuelled towboat. Because it had a very shallow draft and could winch itself over portages it was very useful on the lakes and rivers that fed into the big lake. *(Archives of Ontario)*

The alligator boat was somewhat revolutionary. It was the first tow boat that could pull itself over a portage by its own power—the power of her winch, aided by logs that were placed under it to act as rollers. The alligator had a steam engine, fuelled by wood. The crew consisted of one captain, a wheelsman, two engineers, two deckhands, and four boomsmen. In addition they had a rowboat with a crew of six bringing up the rear of the boom and loosening it wherever it might get caught on points, rocks, or islands. Around the clock they were on duty, working for six hours and resting for six. So in effect, the total crew required was double the number stated above, a complement of thirty-two men. Archie towed and drove logs over that route until 1932, when all the timber operations in Kipawa closed down.

Just a word about Archie Perrier. When his father died at an early age Archie was raised by Joe Decontie in Joe's Bay, on Lake Kipawa, just off Sunnyside Farm. His father was of Native heritage and came from Maniwaki, while his mother was a descendant of the

Hunter family that had settled in 1847 at Hunter's Lodge, on Hunter's Lake. Archie and his wife Rose bought the little store that was owned by Isaac Hunter. Isaac cleared the original farm there, giving the place its name, Hunter's Point.

Archie Perrier was a good man, a supporter of all that is decent in humanity, and there is not a person who remembers him who will not bear this out. He lived a life that reflected his high principles and firm beliefs. Though he raised a family of ten children, he always had time for a fellow human being in need. He grubstaked anyone who genuinely needed it, regardless of the fact that there was small hope of being paid back because of the depresson. He gave food to old people, when there were no old age pensions, and he knew they could never repay him. He saw no one go hungry. A stuanch Presbyterian, he never smoked, drank, or swore. His honesty, trust, and reliability were beyond question.

A young fellow who worked for Archie during the latter years of log-driving was Harry Michel. Harry grew up with his family in Wa-shag-amy Bay, a stone's throw from the northeast end of Archie's farm. As a youngster he attended the Indian Day School, finishing grade three or four. At first glance Harry Michel had nothing that would make him stand out. As a matter of fact he was a very shy, retiring individual, usually living the life of a recluse. The paradox of his story is, however, that when he joined the log drive each spring he became aggressive and fearless. White water seemed to ignite a primal excitement with him and he continuously tested his supple, muscular body against the power of the river. It was said of him that he had the agility and sure-footedness of a cat, and that he sometimes used his pike pole like a pole-vaulter, when he leaped from shore to boom, or from one boom to another. Though the stories may be exaggerated, Harry did things in the rapids and on the booms that defied challenge from anyone.

After the lumber business closed down completely in the Kipawa territory, Harry went to work on the log drives for the pulp companies elsewhere. The people of Hunter's Point followed his exploits in the world of white water and logs, as people nowadays follow their hometown heroes in hockey and baseball. One of the stories that people liked to tell about was the time Harry ran the Big Sturgeon Rapids on the Sturgeon River. Apparently he arrived with a drive at the head of the rapids and the logs were already going

Harry Michel.

through, when a couple of Americans sauntered up somewhat fascinated by these risky activities. They asked the foreman if it were possible for anyone to go through those rapids on a log. The foreman pointed to Harry and said, "That fellow, Harry Michel can do it if anybody can." The Americans found that Harry was a bit shy and difficult to approach; being challenged, however, he sprang to the occasion. Harry strode up to the head of the rapid, a distance of about one hundred yards, and chose a large white spruce to ride. Dotted with large boulders, the rapid flowed steep and swift. The speed of the flow and the ridges of submerged boulders posed as the greatest danger. On riding a log you go where the log takes you. Luckily, there were no large swells to sweep him off. However, at one point the log came to a dead stop against a protruding rock. Harry, with the instincts of a cat jumped at the moment of impact. When he came down, his own forward motion on the now stationary log forced him to his knees, but in a flash he was back on his feet. Without any further mishaps he was swept through the white water and into an eddy that took him ashore to where the spectators were waiting. It is doubtful that anyone ever rode a log through that rapid, either before or since. One of the Americans gave him three packs of tailor-made cigarettes for his attempt.

Another feat in which he remained unchallenged was running over a pulp boom across the Ottawa River at Angliers, Quebec. The reason that it was so difficult is that the pulp booms are made up of an assortment of logs running from eight to sixteen feet long. Some of the tops might be as small as three inches in diameter, unable to support a logger. To stay atop the logs, it takes lightning-fast feet, good balance, and good reflexes, not to mention the ability to choose the right path amongst the logs. Harry did this several times over the half mile width of river, and so provided the onlookers an unusual show, free of charge.

When the lumber business wound to a halt in the early thirties it left many people out of work, and once again almost everyone returned to trapping. The seasonal work in the lumber camps and on the drives was really the first introduction to a wage economy experienced by most of the people, and they liked it. In a way it spoiled some of the bushmen, who had previously enjoyed a satisfactory life in the bush, where money didn't mean so much. Rather than their customary way-of-life, they now looked to the trapline for a wage. They were quickly disappointed, for fur prices

Ross Lake Depot lies idle in 1931. *(Courtesy of Hanna Reynolds)*

had sunk to the lowest ever recorded. Many people now lived in the bush, overcrowding the grounds and so reduced the population of the fur-bearing animals. There were still enough moose and fish to ensure survival.

Some fur-buyers preferred not to sell and resorted to storing furs in wooden barrels in hopes that the market would rise again. They were disappointed; prices did not increase again until the outbreak of World War II. During the depression, which lasted from 1929 to 1939, most people in Hunter's Point could afford to buy only the necessities of life from the store; there were no luxuries then. At least, the land provided meat, fish, foul, and berries, ensuring the survival of its people.

This bridge was built across the Ostoboning River, as a relief project, in 1938-39. *(Courtesy Hanna Reynolds)*

Relief projects were carried out in the bush communities at subsistence level wages. One project was the building of a bridge across the Ostoboning River at Hunter's Point; another was the construction of the first gravel highway between Temiscaming and Ville Marie. Workmen's wages were ninety cents a day.

The lumber business was dormant until Booth began construction of a mill at Tee Lake in 1940. Several camps were opened in locations such as Red Pine Chute, Grind Stone Lake, Russell Bay, and later in other places. But, the pine forests would never again command the importance they had in previous years, for what was being cut now were spindly remnants of the luxuriant stands of the previous century.

During the war the number of Native people who worked in the lumber camps were few because every able-bodied man had gone overseas. I worked at Red Pine in 1942, when I was fifteen, and our crew consisted of old men, teen-age boys, and the few young men whom the army had rejected.

CHAPTER NINE

Forest Fire Protection

Forest-fire protection was deemed necessary by the lumber companies to protect their timber stands, as more and more outsiders entered the Kipawa, and other territories of the upper Ottawa River, in the early part of the century. They formed a subsidiary company called the Ottawa River Forest Protective Association Limited to carry out this function.

Being innate conservationists, the Native inhabitants did not need the Association. Over countless centuries they had developed an attitude and a system of fire safety which practically ruled out the possibility of accidental fires made by man. Their system worked fine so long as they were the only people in the bush. But now, many strangers were encroaching on different parts of the territory and the Native people feared that their homelands would go up in smoke. Several serious fires had been caused by negligent strangers. Because the Native people did not want their forest resources burned up, they cooperated with the lumber companies to implant the Association. The age-old Native system of fire protection was effective and simple. Its golden rule was "Don't start any fires and you don't have to fight them." This idea was impressed upon the Association, but not with immediate results. Camp and lunch fires are never made in black muck and peat, or in areas of inflammable material like dry twigs, sticks, or grasses. Instead they are made in rocky, sandy, or gravelly clearings close to the water. Before leaving a fireplace, the earth underneath and around was thoroughly soaked with water to extinguish every spark. If there were any partial wood sticks or embers remaining they were thrown into the water. Native people did burn certain areas, but with a purpose. To burn off the previous year's growth of brush in a garden clearing, fires were often set during the first sunny days of spring when there was no danger of the fire spreading. They also burned islands to refertilize the growth of blueberries.

An ironic occurrence took place shortly after the Ottawa River Forest Protective Association commenced operations in the Kipawa territory. One of the first assistant inspectors employed was a fellow known now only by the name of Burwash. He cooked his lunch over an open fire on Brulé Lake. Having failed to douse his fire completely before leaving the site, he caused what was then one of the worst forest fires in the territory. Whether he was fired is unknown.

Prior to 1915, when the Association was extended to the Kipawa territory, lumber companies arranged individual protection for their timber limits. During the fire hazard seasons of the years 1908 to 1914, Edward Robinson carried out weekly patrols between Ogascanan Lake and Red Pine Chute for McLachlin Brothers Lumber Company. His job was to spot forest fires, then to extinguish and report them. Other individuals carried out similar patrols in different parts of the territory.

In the summer of 1916 Harry Loken, the first inspector for the Association, hired Seymour Robinson of Wolf Lake as a guide for his survey of the area containing Wolf, Ogascanan, and Saseginaga Lakes. They spent much of the summer planning the patrol beats for fire rangers, and for selecting the sites for cabins and fire towers. For spotting fires, the towers were to be built on the highest mountains in the area. This was the beginning of an agency that was to operate and wield significant influence in the territory until its demise from obsolescence in the 1950's.

The Association realized, as did the lumber companies before them, that only the Natives knew all the routes. In enlisting their

Fire Patrol No. 3. This little steel-hulled boat patrolled Lake Kipawa from the Association headquarters in Kipawa village to Red Pine Chute, taking in Sunnyside, Turtle Portage, Butney and occasionally Hay Bay and anywhere else along the Lake Kipawa shoreline it was required to fight fire.

help the Association promised that the local Native people would always be given preference for the work. It was this promise and also a desire on the part of the Native people to protect their forests that brought them to close cooperation with the Association. People like Antoine Endogwen figured prominently. He drew intricate maps of the whole northwest portion of the Kipawa territory for the Association. He drew maps for the fire towers that were so accurate that they were not replaced until the advent of aerial photograph maps. Other Natives were hired to make maps for the rest of the area.

Water was the main ingredient for fighting fires in those days, and the most efficient means of transporting water was a fire pump, a small portable water pump. It became necessary to widen all the trails to enable the men, fire pumps, and equipment to be transported to all bodies of water where the pumps might be used. These trails became known as portages and were so well identified on the maps that strangers would not get lost. Besides being hired to widen the portage trails and to sketch the canoe routes, the Natives were also hired to post signs along the route to indicate the way. Several Native people objected to the widening of their trails and the posting of the routes, feeling that they would make it much too easy for strangers to invade their territories. The Association, the lumber companies, and government officials had all promised that the family hunting territories would be respected. As usual those promises were broken. Of all the "improvements" offered by the Association, the posting of the routes was considered by the Native people the most onerous. Posting meant placing signs at the entrance of each portage and at every point, narrows, and turn along a water route. In fact, when travelling by water you were hardly ever out of sight of one. It made travel so easy that even the most inexperienced stranger could penetrate the heart of the territory. The poster itself was usually a foot-and-a-half square or larger. The colors were bright enough to be seen from great distances. Some bore a message reading, "Help us keep the forest green," or some other homily suitable to foreign travellers.

The installation of a telephone system became another temporary job for Native people. A network of trails had to be cut linking together the various fire towers, ranger camps, and lumber company depots throughout the territory. Some of the lumber company depots were used as headquarters.

After each trail was cut, telephone lines had to be strung. Before stringing the lines, hundreds of rolls of telephone wire had to be transported to convenient locations along the lakes and rivers. Each roll weighed about 250 pounds and was usually shipped around by the canoeload. After they had been taken as far as they could by canoe, they would be portaged (carried singly) by men to designated positions along the telephone trail. To lay out the wire, a six or eight-foot pole was passed through the hub of the roll to act as an axle, and two men carried each roll between them, unrolling and stringing out the wire as they went. The wire was hung ten or twelve feet above the ground and strung through insulators attached to trees or to the posts erected for the purpose. This job was completed in the early 1930's, providing fast communications to all parts of the territory.

Although the Ottawa River Forest Protective Association was a small organization in the eyes of the public and the lumber companies, it had much significance to the Native people, who recognized it as protection against the dangers that came with tourists, lumbermen, and other outsiders. Like all other foreign impositions, however, the more firmly the Association became entrenched, the more colonial its attitude became. And though it seemed insignificant at the time, its colonial attitude has had a far-reaching effect, as witnessed by the opening of canoe and portage routes, which had much to do with the breaking up of the family hunting grounds. Wages were rock-bottom and the maximum season of employment was five months, so that the people who were employed from elsewhere were usually cast-offs from jobs elsewhere.

Although several Native people worked for the Association at first, they were poorly treated, and their disillusionment grew with the passage of the years. Low wages was one reason; that supervisory jobs always went to outsiders was another.

After the territory was well mapped and the routes learned, there was little need for respecting the promises made and so relatives of both the Association and lumber company management were given preference for job openings. The greatest lesson of this experience for Native people is this: no matter how innocent or sincere the purpose of any undertaking on their land might appear, moves instigated by outside interests have invariably served those interests to the detriment of Native people.

CHAPTER TEN

Tourism

The first tourists to visit Kipawa territory, according to archaeological studies, arrived about five thousand years ago. They were the dauntless forefathers of the present-day Native people of the land. In those freshening years, some two thousand years after the icecap had begun to recede, when vegetation and trees were again beginning to attach themselves to the soil and when animals, birds, and fishes were once more finding food and haven in a land of lakes and rivers, man appeared. Bands or family groups of Nishnabi people must have arrived, exploring the new growth at long last beginning to turn the glacial sands into soil, the forests filling with trees, half-grown and uniform in height; and water lilies and marsh grasses filling the shorelines along crystal-clear lakes and sparkling streams. In those pristine times that followed the grinding purification of the icecap, it is possible that the Nishnabi were returning to a homeland from which their ancestors were forced to retreat when the ice age began. We don't know for sure; the icecap wiped the earth clean of whatever evidence there may have been of earlier habitation.

The Nishnabi may have followed a course of travel along the Ottawa River either by canoeing or by following the river banks on foot, depending on whether the birchbark canoe had been invented by that time. The scene is difficult to imagine today. Perhaps bands made up of fifteen or twenty people of all ages—men, women, and children, dressed in furs, wearing moose and deer-hide moccasins, and carrying stone or copper axes, clubs, bows, arrows, and fish spears moved in to the area. They might have carried skins for shelter, rolled up to make packs to carry all their worldy possessions. The pack might have been carried by means of a tumpline, a strap of moose hide cinched around the pack and used as a headstrap for carrying.

Mentioning the birchbark canoe and copper tools touches upon two mysteries of the past. As ancient history is uncovered, we may learn that the canoe and the copper tools have had a very close relationship in shaping North American history. In his book *The Upper Ottawa*

Valley,[22] Clyde C. Kennedy discusses copper artifacts discovered on Morrison and Allumette Islands, near Pembroke, Ontario. The site has been dated as being approximately 4,700 years old. The artifacts were described as "mostly small fishhooks, awls, and gorges (a straight, double-pointed pin-like object used in fishing) but also socketed axes, knives, socketed spearpoints, and conical-shaped spearpoints." He also describes another find at the site: copper needles with eyes, indicating a relatively sophisticated system of heating and fashioning tools for that era. The Allumette Island campsite yielded more than a thousand of these copper artifacts. The copper culture which existed five thousand years ago had the Ottawa River as its main corridor of travel between Lake Superior and the southern Quebec and New England regions. The source of the natural copper were several locations on Lake Superior. Pit mining was done at two of these sites. The Morrison and Allumette Islands residents could have obtained copper either by trading, or by taking trips to Lake Superior. Either meant a great deal of water travel between the upper end of Lake Superior and the Ottawa River by the Georgian Bay and Nipissing route. It's difficult to believe that anyone could have travelled those great distances without some kind of efficient water conveyance. Only the birchbark canoe could have met those requirements five thousand years ago. The fact that the Morrison and Allumette people were island dwellers increases the likelihood that they did use birchbark canoes.[23]

Anthropological studies indicate that these early tourists drifted along, exploring lakes and rivers, curious where they might find more game and fish. They became enveloped in, and part of, the land's ecology. No colonization societies or government subsidies got them located or insured their livelihood. Each summer they probably explored new lands, until finally they came to an area which best suited their needs. Those first tourists became the first settlers. *Thus arrived the founding race.*

From time immemorial traditional family hunting groups had maintained trails between all the lakes, rivers, and ponds of their territory, over which to portage their canoes. In the Nishnabi tongue these portage trails were known as *Onigami*. The canoe was the chief mode of travel, since Kipawa territory falls within that

---

22. P. 35.
23. *Ibid.*, p. 63.

geological formation known as the Canadian Shield. So characteristically the land is endowed with a copious number of lakes and rivers; a land which sometime in the distant past mothered the invention of the birchbark canoe. These canoe routes were connected to those of their neighbours on all sides, creating an endless maze of water routes throughout the territory of Kipawa. This network of routes did not stop at the boundaries of the territory. They linked the regional groups, tribes, and nations throughout the Canadian shield in the same way as it linked the family groups together in Kipawa. Since the system obviously spanned much of Canada from the earliest time, the European claims to discovery, to exploration, and to its theory of two founding races simply becomes idiotic.

This system of interconnecting travel routes revives the question of precontact—and pre-epidemic—population of the indigenous peoples. Although, as I stated in chapter three, it is impossible to accurately fix the number of people alive at the time of European contact, it is possible to make a reasonable estimate. One method was shown in chapter three: basing a guess on the travellers' accounts and missionaries' records of the time. Another method is more direct: basing an estimate on the land's ability to support a hunting, fishing, and gathering society. The starting point might be the population of family hunters and gatherers that the land would be capable of supporting.

At first, it is tempting to suppose that the maximum population estimate is safe; there was a time in which the amount of meat, fish, berries, and other natural foods was greater than it is now. Furthermore, this was the main factor; firearms and foreign diseases played no part in the fluctuation of the Native population before firearms were introduced. Nevertheless, the availability of the food supply does vary from year to year; droughts do occur, and there is no way of knowing the toll indigenous diseases took on Native or game populations in precontact times. The safest rule, therefore, is what Justus von Liebeg called the Law of the Minimum, which states that an organism's growth and survival is limited by the essential material that is present in the lowest quantity.[24] Therefore, a guess

---

24. From John Bodley, *Anthropology and Contemporary Human Problems*, p. 63.

123

should not be made of the *highest* population that will be sustained by the environment at any one time, but of the highest population that can be sustained *continuously* by that environment.

More research is needed to estimate by that method what the original population might have been; it will involve knowledge of the potential yield of game, fish, and plant foods that were consumed by the Native population at the time. Let us assume, however, that the population in Kipawa territory was then as it is today: 1,250. Since the local population has increased since the epidemics, there is some justification of this supposition. Furthermore, since many Natives from Kipawa have left in search of better opportunities elsewhere, this may be a conservative estimate.

Assuming this figure, given that Kipawa territory covers eight thousand square kilometers, and given that the greater northern hunting area of Canada is roughly 4,400,000 square kilometers, or 550 times the area of Kipawa territory, we can estimate that the population of the hunting territory of Canada at large was 687,500 (multiplying 1,250 by 550). Of course, to qualify this figure, it will be necessary to take into account the different social and hunting customs as well as harvesting capacities, which change by geographical location, terrain, and climate. All these studies are imperative if Native Canadians are ever to discover their genuine roots.

The second wave of tourism, with which we now deal, began shortly after the Canadian Pacific Railway reached Temiskaming in 1894. Those twin steel lines signalled the grand entrance of colonialsim into the Kipawa territory. In the beginning the tourists who came north were considerate and easy to accommodate. The land was remote and uncharted; there were no bush highways or aircraft to take them beyond the end of the steel. It was necessary to go by canoe, and tourist hunters dared not venture into the bush without a guide. It was all hard work both on the part of the guide and the hunter alike. The guide provided the expertise; he was also the conservationist, ensuring that moose hides were not wasted and that all the meat was brought out of the bush. This sometimes meant carrying meat and hide over many portages. If the tourist hunter did not want the meat, the guide smoked it for his own use. In either event, in keeping with the tradition of the land and its people, the guide never wasted meat.

A freighter canoe setting out for Kipawa from Hunter's Point. Aboard are a couple of hunters; the antlers and meat of the moose killed is towed in the canoe behind. *(Courtesy Hanna Reynolds)*

Moose hunting on Saseginaga Lake. *(Courtesy of Doris Hansen)*

The earliest oral account that I recorded about so called sports goes back to about 1910. In those times it seems that Americans and a few Europeans occasionally rode to the end of the CPR rails at Temiscaming, looking for adventure in the shape of a giant moose or a bear. After a few of those would-be hunters ended up on the door step of the Station Agent for the CPR, he got in touch with Frank Jawbone, a well-known bushman who lived in the vicinity of the present-day village of Kipawa. At the time there was a wagon road from Temiscaming to Kipawa, and the teamsters working for the lumber companies hauled all their supplies by horse and wagon. Frank received the message from one of the teamsters.

He agreed to guide these stray hunters for a daily wage and in time built up a lively clientele. For a while the CPR was in the business of making arrangements for hunting trips between tourists and guides. These free and easy arrangements lasted only until the early 1920's.

Compare those early days, when tourist and guide were able to experience a closeness to the land, with today's scene: beer cans, garbage, slaughtered animals and fish, lakes polluted from high-powered motors and senseless dumpage. Consider the laws making possible this devastation: open season to shoot cows and calf moose, and allowing the penetration to the very heartland of their breeding grounds during the mating season when the moose are most vulnerable. Consider the idiots on snowmobiles in winter, chasing animals to death to satisfy their demented minds. Consider the drunken "sportsmen" shooting high-powered rifles for the pleasure of maiming animals for which they have no real need or interest. Consider these; then decide whether this is civilization!

Wealthy Americans drawn north by the allure of wilderness hunting of big game, in the 1920's, created an increased demand for guides and equipment. Store keepers became outfitters. They came by this naturally, since they knew all the trappers from everyday dealings, and they provided provisions and equipment for the bush. Archie Perrier and Garfield Jones became outfitters in Hunter's Point, while Robbie Cunningham outfitted in Kipawa. Licenses had become a requirement and only bull moose could be shot.

Gradually, tourist fishing created a similar demand for guides and outfitting. Pickerel and pike were abundant in those days and many of the good trout lakes had barely been fished. There were some

Edward Perrier and Lawrence Boudrias with a bear they shot. 1938. *(Courtesy Doris Hansen)*

exceptional trophies. One client of Archie Perrier's came out from Qui-wi-chi lake with three trout that together weighed one hundred pounds. Stories of lake trout weighing up to forty-five pounds were heard from time to time.

Tourism increased into the 1930's and early 1940's, but the nature of the work and the seasons involved, provided the guides with temporary work at best. They might have three weeks worth of

A party of moose hunters very early in the century. Six American hunters and six guides. Mike Jawbone is pictured on the extreme right. *(Archives of Ontario)*

guiding in the spring. In the summer they could expect a month's worth of fishing trips and three weeks work guiding moose hunters in the fall. But as anyone who has lived through the depression knows, any chance to earn a few dollars in those days was better than nothing.

Occasionally big-game hunters came from Europe. In 1938, the year prior to the outbreak of war, a party of twenty-one hunters came from Germany under the auspices of the CPR. They were outfitted by Garfield Jones in Hunter's Point. The trip was somewhat bizarre for the times. War preparations were now underway, and the propaganda machines on both sides were working overtime to justify the impending disaster. Between the two world wars practically everything we heard or read about German people had a fearful or antagonistic slant. No wonder the local people were curiously suspicious about those strangers. The guides generally agreed, however, that the Germans were good hunters and fine gentlemen. Moose were scarce at the time and only three of the twenty-one hunters got a moose.

Immediately following World War II the tempo of tourist fishing began to pick up. This came about for several reasons, and the new affluence of the working man in the United States was not the least of them. Another was the new gravel road that allowed easy access to the shores of Lake Kipawa. Fishermen were able to obtain maps and charts of the whole territory; no longer did they have to hire guides. The tourists brought in their own boats and motors, campers, trucks, trailers, food supplies, gas, and booze.

In 1968 I witnessed one sign of this influx. A group of moose hunters equipped with two trucks fed an insane desire of theirs to get to the heart of the moose country. On one truck they carried a portable plank bridge that could be set up to cross any stretch which the lumber companies had previously bridged, and left the piers. They travelled with many of the conveniences of home but they acted like an army out to make war on the moose. Even most of their equipment was army surplus. This was the result: a tiny bear cub, whose body had been ripped to shreds by a high-powered bullet, lay on the ground in front of their camp.

From the end of the 1940's to the 1960's thousands of fishermen flocked into the territory of Kipawa. Many new outfitters got into the business. Tourist operators built camps in every known area of good fishing. Flying-in became the most popular and easy way to get to the isolated lakes. They had the better places to fish until those lakes ultimately met the fate of all lakes that are easy to get to. The lower lakes deteriorated, but fishermen still came in droves to the easily accessible regions.

In years past the residents of Kipawa had fished for much of their food in the lower lakes; in the fall seasons of the early 1940's we used to tow booms of birch stove wood across the lake, a distance of two to four miles. While towing we would troll with a line and spoon and catch enough trout—two or three—for our own needs. They usually ranged from five to ten pounds in weight, providing a good share of the protein for the families who lived along the lake. Now, trout are seldom caught in that part of the lake.

Earlier I showed how the scarcity of animal life, and especially the fur-bearing animals, had affected the lives of the people from the early 1920's onward. The decline in the game population persisted until the 1950's. This brings up the question why tourists would want to come to an area where game was so scarce. One immediate answer is the fact that the tourists who visited the Kipawa territory in

Joe McKenzie, one of the few native outfitters of Kipawa. *(Courtesy Charlie McKenzie)*

the 1920's and 1930's probably amounted to no more than one per cent of the tourist flow of the 1960's and 1970's. There are other historic reasons, however, which deal with the scarcity of wildlife in earlier years and also its revival in the latter years, which are worth repeating here.

During the war and afterwards, a majority of the bush people moved to communities like Kipawa, Temiscaming, and Belleterre. Some still trapped and hunted from those locations, while others turned to lumbering, mining, and other local industries. This lessened the pressures on the land considerably. The territory had been overhunted and overtrapped during the depression years by the Native people, and also by outsiders. Paying no heed to conservation practices of the Native people, outsiders killed everything they could. In desperation the Native trappers abandoned their traditional methods of conservation, for any stock they left for breeding would only be poached by outsiders.

When Chief Shene and his companions journeyed to Ottawa in the early 1920's, with the hope of reserving hunting territories for the

Native residents, he had foreseen the possible consequences of killing more than the land could reproduce. Food problems were already apparent to the people living from the land's natural produce. He had hoped to return the land to its previous stability so that the families could conserve their food supplies. As will be recalled, he failed.

The situation had worsened when the Ottawa River Forest Protective Association posted all the routes and opened the portages to the general public. Many people from outside came to the bush to survive. They came with the belief that *the land was open and uninhabited*, a common myth fostered by the colonial mentality of this country. Many hunters knew no more about trapping and hunting than they had read in books. A hunter can be totally unskilled, however, and still be able to kill big game with a high-powered rifle, and many relied on this weapon to survive. Animals like moose and bear present a good target at three or four hundred yards, but the lack of shocking power and the probability of being off target at that distance contributes to the wounding of many animals—animals who later die, never to be found. Although some of the strangers did use much of the moose and deer that they shot, others left as many behind to rot. The Native people had sympathy for the poor people who poached to survive. Respect for life has always been an intrinsic part of their spiritual and cultural beliefs. Those sympathies, unfortunately, worked to their own detriment in the end, a common lesson in the colonization of the country.

I had grown up with only the stories of how families once managed their own land, and how much better it was in those days when each family conserved its own animals. Although I had not experienced those better times, I realized how much worse things had become in my time. My last year as a trapper was in the winter of 1942 and 1943. My father and I travelled 125 miles east from Hunter's Point to the headwaters of the Black and Coulonge Rivers, only to find no more than ten families of beaver. In the old days, the family preserves had produced ten families of beaver in five miles of watershed. We had travelled by canoe and by snowshoe; there were no snowmobiles then. Now, there was not a single moose to be found in our trapping area for the fall's meat supply. Animal life in the territory had probably reached its lowest ebb since the ice age. By then only a few families remained in the bush. The villages of Hunter's Point, Wolf Lake, and Brennan Lake had been considerably reduced. By the end of the 1940's the number of people who now hunted and trapped regularly probably dropped to no more than twenty per cent of what it had been during the Depression. The wildlife began to revive, slowly at first, but with great resiliency in the 1950's. By the 1960's wildlife had probably returned to a population close to the state of equilibrium maintained by family group conservation.

There were several reasons for the resurgence of game during the 1940's and 1950's. To begin with, the depressed prices for furs discouraged many families from trapping during the late 1930's. During World War II, most of the men left the community to fight overseas or to work in the war industries, leaving few to trap for a living. Then, after World War II, the trapline system was set up, leaving plots too small for any family to make a living by trapping.

Thus as game increased in the 1950's and 1960's, tourism also increased from the USA. The working class had reached a measure of affluence that allowed them to vacation in far-flung places, and technology made the hinterland of Kipawa an easy target. As tourism increased so did the intervention of the Ministry of Tourism, Game, and Fish. Unfortunately, the legislation and policies of that Ministry appeared to have no other purpose than to make the area as easily accessible as it could to the maximum number of tourists and thereby reap maximum financial returns, while at the same time totally disregarding the needs of the people of the land. Evidence for this policy will be covered in chapters twelve and thirteen.

CHAPTER ELEVEN

The Move from the Communities

In the 1930's and the 1940's, there began a migration of Natives from the outlying communities—Hunter's Point, Brennan Lake, Wolf Lake, and elsewhere—to Kipawa and communities outside Kipawa territory. There were several reasons for this migration—depletion of game in the bush, limited job opportunities, and, after the start of World War II, emigration of the males to the battlefield overseas or the war factories in the cities. This chapter traces the history of this migration.

Prior to the outbreak of World War II living conditions in the hinterland communities were at their worst. The effect of poachers and the immense pressure caused by the depression years on the land began to tell. Fur prices were extremely low and no one knew whether those prices reflected the true state of the market, or had been artificially set to make money for the fur buyers to the extreme disadvantage of the trapping families. To subsist, the trappers were forced to catch more and more furs from among an ever diminishing number of animals.

During the summer months there was a government bounty of ten dollars on bears, which benefited few, since bears were scarce. To grace the palates of rich patrons of the Waldorf-Astoria Hotel in New York City, there was also a market for fish. Pickerel and pike brought three cents a pound, while trout sold for four cents. The fish were caught with hand lines. Since the fish agent feared that gill netting might produce stale fish, that method of catching fish was unacceptable. Commercial fishing by troll had little or no effect on the lakes' supply of fish. Trolling for fish meant that they were caught only when they were biting, saving the fish population at least. Commercial seine fishing had been carried out earlier in the century, but lost out through competition from large fishing operations in the Great Lakes, which contained larger supplies of fish and involved less distance to market the catch. Nevertheless, many caught a good portion of their food supplies with gill nets.

Some people had their gardens and livestock to fall back on, but the fur income decreased as time when on. Those who followed the ancient tradition of living almost exclusively on country food were faring no better. By then some species of animal life were nearing extinction, and the population of all animals was down. The plea by the Native people to have their traditional family hunting grounds recognized by government still fell on deaf ears, and the natural methods of conservation, that had evolved through countless generations, were swept aside to serve the interests of the colonial masters.

Small wonder that most of the people from Hunter's Point, Brennan Lake, and Wolf Lake moved to the village of Kipawa. It was a compromise of sorts. They could find jobs, yet remain in touch with their land. Some moved to Temiscaming or North Bay, while others moved northward to Belleterre, Rouyn/Noranda, and Val d'Or.

The Department of Indian Affairs played a significant role in persuading the traditional hunting families to move from Hunter's Point and other places to Kipawa village. Other than to centralize school and other services, it is not clear why Indian Affairs desired this move. The move brought into Kipawa people ill-prepared for the work-a-day world. In the winter of 1978 some families expressed a desire to move back to the bush communities since they were unhappy with conditions in Kipawa. Two problems involved with moving back were:

(1) the takeover of their trapping grounds by outsiders;
(2) the deprivation of their children of an education.

Another peculiarity exists with regard to government attitude towards Native people: the County government has attempted to tax bush people for homes they left behind in Hunter's Point in the way they tax foreigners for summer homes. For the registered "Indians" who live in Kipawa their homes in Hunter's Point are not a luxury; they are the only homes they own. The homes they occupy on the reserve are owned by the Band. Those who maintain homes in Hunter's Point do so for security, like an insurance policy. If it becomes necessary to move back to Hunter's Point and to live from the land again, the people have at least a house to move to.

The focus of the latter part of this book is on Kipawa village, because it represents exploitation and alienation to which Native people have been subjected. These are microcosms of what has happened to indigenous people under colonial rule everywhere in the

Pat Robinson, one of the very splendid, old-time trappers and hunters of other years. Pat and most of his family now live in Kipawa, they moved there from Hunter's Point in the 1960's.

A cabin home in Hunter's Point.

world. Of the approximately 1,250 descendents of the original people of Kipawa territory, more than four hundred lived in the village of Kipawa, while a few might be found scattered across this country. Since they lack the education and the opportunity to be part of the privileged class, none are rich. Many belong to the ordinary, blue-collar society. They go to work day after day and don't fall into the stereotype of "Indian" that we hear so much about; they are never mentioned. Then, there are a few who have ended up on skid row in Toronto, Winnipeg, and Vancouver. These are the ones whom TV cameras pan once in a while to show how bad things are for the original Canadians.

The people who moved to Kipawa cleared land and built homes along the lakeshore, as had been their custom, on both sides of the bay leading into Gordon Creek. Canoes and boats were still much in use, for there were no roads. Everyone used wood for cooking and heating; so, little booms of birch and dry pine for winter wood were commonly seen being towed in during the fall. Those houses that were built in the 1940's and 1950's were of log and frame construction, no doubt lacking in the quality of insulation that is on the market today; nevertheless the workmanship of those houses was of the highest standard. Many of the bush people were jacks-of-all-trades who built their own homes with the help of a neighbor or neighbors. By custom most of the Native inhabitants left good spaces for garden pasture between themselves and their next-door neighbors. In Kipawa village they might just as well have forgotten that custom. For the most part the land is unfit for gardening, being mostly bedrock with a thin layer of topsoil covering it.

When the people moved to the village, in any event, they did so intending to change their ways of life. Booth Lumber Limited had a new mill at Tee Lake and for a while there was plenty of work in the lumber camps, on log drives, on boom-towing operations on Lake Kipawa, and on log-sorting operations on Gordon Creek and Tee Lake, all of which fed the mill. Then there was work in the mill itself, in the lumber yard, and in construction. However, as in most resource-exploitation industries, there is usually a short period of boom and a longer period of bust.

Those who combined trapping with seasonal work for the companies followed a course of action that was practical for a man whose heart remained in the bush. Men like Barney Jawbone captained tow boats for Booth Lumber every summer then trapped every winter. Every working man in Kipawa, together with some of the women, worked for Booth at one time or another. Eventually, those who worked in lumber for a living found themselves out of work when the pine operations declined, and again when heavy equipment replaced men in the bush.

After World War II, men returned from overseas only to find that a greater distance had to be travelled to get to the trapping grounds in the territory that still contained any game. They also discovered that the 1947 law requiring registering of traplines all but eliminated their livelihood. Consequently, they joined the others who had already settled in the village of Kipawa.

When the people began building in Kipawa, few gave any thought to acquiring title to the land; for them, it was unheard of. The ancient code of the bush—that when a man cleared land for his home and garden it was his—remained in force in their minds. Not until after several families had already built in 1944 were the men working for Booth Lumber informed that they had built on Gordon Creek Improvement land. The advice was given by an employee of Booth, and it was explained that the Gordon Creek Improvement Company was a subsidiary of three companies: Booth Lumber, Canadian International Paper, and a third one no longer remembered locally. Its purpose was to improve the waterways in order to pass logs through Gordon Creek to the Ottawa River.

Booth Lumber's reluctance to inform the people that they were on leased properties probably stemmed from two factors. First, they suspected that the people on these properties knew nothing of land title; second, those people doing the building comprised a good part of the company's work force and for the sake of good work relations the company handled the matter delicately. When the employees of Booth were informed that their homes were on company land, they were advised not to worry, since Booth Lumber had put no value on the land. Further the company stated it would relinquish its interest when the log drives ended. Each man was asked to come around to the office to sign a contract and pay a dollar a year for rental.

Unfortunately, Booth Lumber's interest, as well as its promise, has since changed hands. The company was sold to Goodman-Staniforth, who later sold to Universal Oil Products Company (UOP) of Des Plaines, Illinois. UOP in turn sold Gordon Creek

Improvement to a land speculator identified as Mr. Ngwiri. This is the speculator who is now demanding the ten thousand dollars for each lot as outlined in chapter one.

No one really questioned this dollar-a-year ritual, until the village was hit by a bomb, in the form of a letter sent to Edward (Ted) Mongrain, in 1973. Briefly it said that Canadian International Paper Company, one of the parent companies of Gordon Creek Improvement, had sold the land that included Mongrain's house, to Kipawa Air Service Inc. CIP's behaviour as a corporate citizen, had already become seriously questioned by the community because of the manner in which that company had closed the Temiscaming Mill in 1972. Ted was given a choice of buying his lot for five thousand dollars or leasing it for $150.00 a year. He had cleared this land, a very rocky three thousand square foot plot located next to his father's, when he returned from the war and built a small home.

Ted based his challenge on several grounds. First he felt that the CIP had no right to sell the land. Second, he could not understand on what basis a multi-national company was granted the right to speculate on the land that it had acquired for the purpose of floating logs through the river, especially in view of the fact that the company had stripped the timber limits of all useful wood. Third, he felt even more strongly about his aboriginal rights. His Native ancestry had lived in and around the area long before recorded history. Frank Jawbone, his maternal grandfather, had preceded his father in occupying the same general area, and no one knows how many generations before him. His own father, Roch Mongrain, had lived in this very clearing for over sixty years.

The second bomb came a short time later when Mary, the widow of Roch Mongrain, and Ted's mother, was served with a similar letter from Kipawa Air Service's legal representative. To remain in her own home, she would have to pay Kipawa Air Service Inc. eight thousand dollars for the lot, or $150.00 a year. Similar intimidating clauses were contained in the letter. One read: "This lease can be annulled at the end of each year with a thirty day notice and it will not be renewed annually but will have to be discussed every year before a new signature." Another read, "You have ten days to give Kipawa Air Service your opinion regarding this new deed to be signed." It doesn't take much imagination to understand how shocking this letter was to an elderly, Native woman; a woman

Roch Mongrain, sitting at the extreme left, with his Company, the 117th in World War I. He saw action in the trench warfare in France. *(Courtesy Suzie Robinson)*

whose right to live on her own land had never before been questioned.

Needless to say, Mrs. Mongrain did not have the money to pay the eight thousand dollars, nor the ability to put out $150.00 a year from her old-age pension. Roch had spent the major part of his working life for Booth Lumber Limited, but had received no pension for his years of faithful service. The house that Roch built in 1953 replaced an older one of forty years, where his six children had grown up. When Mary and Roch first built in their tranquil, sheltered little bay they looked forward to enjoying their declining years in the company of their children and granchildren. That was not to be. First, the highway arrived, practically cutting through their back yard. Then a government dock was built for tourists next door and, finally, a seaplane base was established. The house was the only thing of material value that Roch had left behind. Some people might contend that Mary Mongrain was dealt with justly since neither her father, her husband, nor her grandfather had sought title to the land. The big question, is of course, whose justice—Native or foreign?

That question has never been debated in the courts, let alone settled. And whose land was it? Mary died shortly afterwards, and the lot and house were left to her daughter, Suzie, who lives in North Bay. The question of ownership has not yet been resolved.

Ted sought help from the Laurentian Alliance of Métis and non-status Indians in Montreal. The Alliance in turn placed the case in the hands of the legal firm of Geoffrion, Prud'homme, Chevrier, Cardinal, Marchessault, Mercier & Greenstein.

The case was settled in accordance with Chapter 322 of the Constitute Tenure System Act. Under the Act, if the lessee has built a structure of greater value than the lot itself, he must be given the first option to buy. The Act included a formula whereby the lessee must pay an amount equal to the annual assessment, retroactive to the date of the original occupancy. The Alliance paid $1,819.27 in legal services and court costs. Ted paid $20.00 for his title. This resolution was applicable in Ted's case because his lease did not contain a valuation of the lot. Where a value is stated on the lease the above remedy does not apply. The original lease issued by Gordon Creek Improvement to the Métis families did not state a land value. Thus, there is a remedy at law through application of Constitute Tenure System Act for those families who still have the original lease. In later years the Company inserted a blanket value of twenty thousand dollars on each contract, regardless of the size or quality of each lot.

Factors which affected the people of Kipawa are only now being locally analyzed and defined. To this point in history the people have remained compliant and even cooperative with the forces of institutional manipulation and control that have led to their near disintegration. The brainwashing through generations is a hindrance that must be reckoned with. However, the threat of expulsion hanging over their heads have brought people to the full realization of the rapacity of the system, together with the dangers of continued outside domination and control. A brief review of Kipawa's history leads one to the obvious conclusion that the present situation has come about because the system has always been exploitative in nature and manipulated from afar. The challenge to the people of Kipawa is to determine by what means they will regain control of their land and their destiny. This is a challenge for all of the indigenous people of the territory, for it is not only a housing lot that is their heritage, over which they should be asserting their rights—it is the Kipawa territory—their homeland and traditional hunting grounds within the nation of the Nishnabi.

Our people are now asking, "What must we do to survive?" In light of past experience, that is the most critical of questions. Survival of the Nishanbi culture will probably depend upon how hard we are willing to work and fight to regain our freedom and dignity. Justice is never gained without a fight; it is not in the nature of human beings to bestow justice. It must be obtained through struggle, at considerable cost.

This land, its inhabitants, human and animal, and its resources have been raped for financial gain; this rape goes on today. The time has come for the Native people of Kipawa to take a stand and secure the soil from which we grew. This is our heritage, our reason for living. If we do not find the determination now it may be lost forever.

CHAPTER TWELVE

Hunting and Fishing Rights Versus Zone d'Amenagement et de Conservation

One bane to Native hunting territories has been private hunting clubs. For many years prior to 1978 individuals and groups had been able to obtain hunting grounds for private hunting and fishing in the province of Quebec. Money and politics were the chief motivators in the acquisition of those special privileges. The original charters were said to have been good for ninety-nine years, and the first clubs came into existence in the Kipawa territories in the 1920's. The lessees were usually rich Americans who could afford to pay for exclusive hunting and fishing rights.

At the time that these leases were consumated, the Native hunters whose grounds were being absorbed, complained, but could find no one with whom a complaint could be lodged. The owners and the government members, with whom they made the deals, lived in far-off places and couldn't be reached. The wardens who kept the Natives from trapping on that land spoke of their bosses as if they possessed mystical powers—beyond reproach in their decrees. Being ignorant of the system and powerless to do anything about it, the Native trapper had no choice but to accept some phrase like "It's the law," or "The Government leased the land," as an explanation.

The Native trappers received absolutely nothing in exchange for the territories which had been taken to establish these exclusive clubs. And strangely enough not even the clergy, who had considerable political power at the time, would take up the cause of the Native trapper. They preached of injustice in far-flung places, but failed to recognize it at home, especially where the evil concerned Native people. The Indian Agent always remained strangely aloof when aboriginal rights were at stake. In light of Shene's treatment in Ottawa, in 1920, the wresting of Native land by any means other than legal, seemed to be the policy of Indian Affairs.

The trapper could take a job as a game warden or as a guide with the newly formed club or go elsewhere, for his land had now become the domain of someone of wealth and influence, residing in New York, Philadelphia, or Chicago. For reasons never understood, the owners of these clubs acquired the rights to fur-bearing animals, as well as to those of hunting and fishing. Without the exercise of conscience on the part of either the politician or the new lord, the Native found himself deprived of his home, his land, and his livelihood. If he accepted work from this new master of the territory, subservience became imperative.

In 1978 the Quebec government abolished all exclusive hunting and fishing rights of private clubs in the province. By the same legislation, however, a new system of clubs was established, once again based on privilege, station in life, and race. The announcement stated that these new regulations were aimed at giving greater priorities and responsibilities to the citizens of Quebec in the management, conservation, and utilization of the province's fishing and wildlife resources.

The new system divided the province into approximately fifty zones, *Zones d'Amenagement et de Conservation* (ZAC) each with an approximate area of three thousand sqaure miles. These larger zones are divided into smaller ones called *Zones Exploitation et de Conservation* (ZEC). These zones are said to vary in size from five hundred to two thousand square miles, and for the purpose of conservation and wildlife management, are under the jurisdiction of local non-profit groups and organizations.

Established groups are given priority by the government, especially outdoor organizations affiliated with the *Federation de la Faune du Quebec*. County councils, chambers of commerce, and outfitters' associations are examples of the other groups that can be chosen to administer ZEC areas.

The ZAC sector within which Kipawa lies extends as far east as La Verendry Park, as far north as the head of Lake Temiskaming and south to where the Dumoine River empties into the Ottawa. This in effect takes in all of the Kipawa territory.

When the new system was announced it was stated that in keeping with government policy the membership and executive of any organization assuming jurisdiction of a ZEC must be composed of a majority of Quebec citizens. Whether by oversight or by design, the first citizens of Quebec were considered neither before nor after the inception of this new system.

The Native people were not consulted at any stage of the development of the *Zones d'Amenagement et de Conservation*, nor have they been invited to participate in any way. As a direct result, Natives will be barred from entering the bush, for the reason that all the areas not presently designated as parks will become clubs for a new privileged group of people. Neo-colonialism strikes again.

The only comparable situation exists in South Africa. To compare the situation at Kipawa with that of South Africa may seem exaggerated at the moment. But consider the potential danger to the Natives of Kipawa if this so called system of Zone Conservation is put into practice throughout the territory.

In South Africa the government has moved to settle all Africans in "homelands" or bantustans. These are the poorest lands. Every African in South Africa over the age of sixteen must carry a pass. It bears his or her name, identity number, ethnic group, employer's name and address, and details of taxes and levies paid. Failure to produce the pass on demand, or possessing a pass lacking any of the requisite stamps, is an offence. The pass permits the holder to enter the cities and industrial areas for work, but only for that purpose. The movement between homeland and work of every black individual is regulated by the white authorities; thus ensuring and perpetuating a system of slavery.

The analogy in Kipawa works somewhat in reverse. In South Africa the official policy is to isolate the African in his so called homeland. In Kipawa the attempt is to isolate the Native from his homeland. If this system is carried to its logical conclusion it will create the following situation:

(1) Access to the lands will be controlled by outsiders.
(2) Permits will have to be obtained from the club administrators, who will issue permits only if it serves the club's interest, or other reasons of external origin.
(3) If a Native is caught on his homeland without a permit, he will be punished by laws that are alien to his person and to his land—treated as a foreigner on his own land.
(4) The policing and control of the land will be done under the guise of conservation. In South Africa this practice is called apartheid.

What is to be done about this situation? Much. This matter obviously has to be taken up with the Government of Quebec. If the Native people of Kipawa themselves do not take the initiative, they face deprivation from the essentials of life itself. Among the steps to be taken are:

(1) The boycott of the ZAC system and the creation of resistance by every means: civil disobedience in severe forms; "trespassing" the areas designated as ZAC; and by obstruction.
(2) Formation and operation of a ZEC club of Native people in what remains of the Kipawa territory; or demand a larger area reserved for Native people; or both.
(3) Request for membership in the ZEC's operating in the territory.
(4) Negotiation for hunting and fishing rights in the broader context of aboriginal rights with the aim of removing these clubs.

CHAPTER THIRTEEN

The Trapline System

One of the fondest myths harbored by the Government of Quebec is that the trapline system is a conservation measure. While it is true that the wildlife population has increased since the establishment of the trapline system in 1947, it has been done at the expense of the livelihood among the Native peoples themselves. Long before the invasion of white settlers, the Natives had developed conservation methods that ensured their livelihood and the preservation of the animals they hunted. They had to; if the Native people extinguished their game, they would have extinguished themselves. Although the trapline may have led to the conservation of game—and that point is debatable—it has effectively ended the traditional livelihood of Native people. This chapter traces the course of the trapline system's development.

Until the turn of the century, each family referred to their territory as home. They had shelters and camp sites at various points from which to hunt and fish in a balanced way. By custom a family harvested a quarter or a fifth of their territory each year to allow the animal life in the remaining area to regenerate. So, a family would be away from any one territory, depending upon its size, for four or five years. The land was allowed to regenerate in the same manner as a farmer leaves selected fields to lie fallow.

It was these preserves that migrant trappers and poachers attacked. In their ignorance of the original hunting system, these interlopers claimed that the land they were hunting was open, since no one was apparently hunting it. In 1920, Chief Shene had attempted to explain natural conservation and the family hunting system to Indian Affairs in Ottawa, but the government ignored his words. By so doing the government condoned and supported the actions of the migrant trappers and poachers, which in turn contributed greatly to the destruction of the original conservation system and the family hunting economy in the territory.

As shown earlier, the entire territory was the home of the hunting family, their shelter, their food, their social, economic and spiritual way of life. There was nothing of their existence that did not emanate from their own land. That feeling of unity with the earth normally finds its meaning in the following expression: "The Land and the People are as one." This simple truth seems incomprehensible to the non-Native.

It was this closeness to the land that made Native people free and independent. The colonizers recognized this characteristic of the Native people from the beginning, and the early forces of imperialism worked constantly to break this independence. The so called early explorers used the technique of claiming all the land in the name of king, queen, or emperor. From a commercial standpoint the fur traders attempted to control by making the people dependent on the goods they exchanged for furs. When this method failed, other forces were brought into play; the Hudson's Bay Company gained early success in this respect. By securing the Royal Charter and the military support of empire, they were virtually able to dictate the lives of people over huge tracts of land. A classic example of the use of imperial force was that used to wage war on the Métis of Red River in 1869. When the Hudson's Bay Company's dominance and control of the Métis people of Red River began to fail, a Canadian Army, comprised of Canadian volunteers and British Regulars, were sent to put down a provoked uprising. The Métis, these settlers of the prairies, had requested nothing more than the recognition of ownership over their land, the freedom to sell furs to whomever they pleased, and the right to determine their own lives.

Whether they were cognizant of it or not, the missionaries, both Catholic and Protestant, followed their own particular plan of colonial control. These mechanisms alienated the spiritual traditions of the people, placing them in an inferior position in a religion that was formulated to suit the needs of other people in other lands. The teachings were ostensibly to better the position of the converts in the Great Hereafter, but, by instruction and by example, the teachings in fact taught and demanded subservience to a European master. Such teachings destroyed people's morale to resist colonial control making them slaves. These teachings probably ranked second in importance to the great epidemics in destroying the morale of the people and distorting the Native self-image and identity.

On the enslavement of people's minds there is a profound lesson to be learned by studying the influence of church and school on North American societies over the past one hundred years. Many other influences are involved, but those of church and school were the most consistent and pervasive, since they were the shrouded tools of colonial dominance. A few elders today still remember how the clergy once blamed the epidemics on the people who remained "pagan." They had preached that God was unhappy with the people for allowing "pagans" and shamans to live amongst them; he was showing His displeasure by raining disease upon His children.

The epidemics, the fur trade, the lumbermen, the churches, the schools, the influx of tourism, the two world wars, and the manipulation by the government all combined to alienate the homelands from the Native people of Kipawa. Not until recent times however, has a government, the Province of Quebec, succeeded both in law and in fact in making Native people foreigners in their own land. The tools that finally brought about absolute control are the combined forces of the Registered Licensed Traplines System, and the *Zone d'Amenagement et de Conservation*. Both organizations are said to have been necessitated to ensure conservation of wildlife and to allow Quebecers to participate in its management. In reality, however, the policies have been directed toward eliminating Native rights to hunt, trap, and fish as an occupational livelihood or as recreation.

The problems of conservation did not begin in 1947. The decimation of animal life that began in the 1910's and 1920's in the bush had forced the hunting families off their land no less than the destruction of the buffalo forced prairie tribes off theirs. Similarly, the slaughter of the buffalo in the plains, and of the game and fur-bearing animals of the territory of Kipawa, was brought about by attitudes held by the Europeans, not those held by the Natives. The attitude of the migrant, foreign poacher, reinforced by the government, led to the overkilling. Without the slightest regard for the family whose territory he plundered, the outsider moved in to poach family preserves he could reach. Since his overpowering objective was to kill every animal he found, he remained in a given area only so long as it was profitable to do so. Because he had no relationship to the land and cared less for its future, he would then move on to ravage other grounds. On the other hand, the Native had always left enough animals for the propagation during the interval that he would be hunting other parts of his territory. These conservation practices of the Native began to break down when it was realized that leaving several "seed" animals amounted to an invitation for the poachers to invade.

These encroachments often led to violent confrontations over hunting grounds. As more strangers moved in, the pressure on the land came close to the breaking point. The Grand Lake Indians, whose territory borders the Kipawa territory to the northeast, had similar problems. After several fatalities of unknown cause and the intercession of the Oblate fathers, the Grand Lake Indian Hunting Reserve was created in 1928. The reserve benefitted a few of the Kipawa families, since the reserve encompassed their grounds and so afforded them official protection. Those grounds outside the reserve, however, faced increased pressure from poachers, for now the land that they could freely plunder was smaller. As a result, many people in the territory remaining in Kipawa began to hunt as indiscriminately as white poachers. Under the combined pressure of indiscriminate hunting and poaching, reinforced by the depression, the unprotected hunting grounds in Kipawa were ravaged, driving every fur-bearing species and game animal nearly to extinction.

Not until the outbreak of the Second World War did the land have some chance to recuperate. From 1939 to 1945, with the removal of most of the able-bodied men to the army or employment in the war industries, fewer people depended on game. When the Ministry of Tourism, Game, and Fish instigated the Registered Trapline System in 1947, the Ministry lacked a true picture of the land and its inhabitants. The animal life now began to recover, but few people had returned to their traditional livelihood at that time. The system was inaugurated without consultation with Native trappers, without consideration to the traditional divisions in the ancestral hunting grounds. In other words, the land was divided randomly into rectangles, squares, and other shapes as if to suit some administrator's whim. Absolutely no regard was given to the watershed, the heights of land, the family hunting territories, or the indigenous methods of conservation. Since the land allotments are too small to provide a livelihood, the system created by the Ministry of Tourism, Game, and Fish caters to people who are already gainfully employed: the recreation hunter and the tourist. By so doing, the traditional homeland of Kipawa's original people has been redesigned as an outsider's playground.

The situation of the Native trappers of Kipawa is illustrated on the following maps. I asked for a map showing the first divisions made by the Ministry of Tourism, Game, and Fish in 1947 together and with the names of individuals who had been allotted the trapping grounds at that time.

I was told by the Temiscaming office of the Ministry that there was no list of individual trappers for that time (this was verified by a phone call to Quebec City), and that the licensed traplines map remains essentially the same as the 1947 copy. It seems that the only important change is that more and more lots are going to non-Natives.

The first map (*Fig. 13.1*) indicates the original family hunting territories that made up the greater part of Kipawa territory. Some of the names are European. There are two known ways that this came about. The first was the adoption of a European name. For instance, the Hudson's Bay Company manager may have found that a Native name was too difficult to pronounce or write so he might have called someone "Paul." So amongst Europeans the individual would be known as Paul, even though he was still known by his own name amongst his own people. Other Natives simply adopted European names on their own accord, for much the same reasons: to be undersood by the manager. When these individuals were christened by priests or ministers, their adopted names became their family names. The second was Native-European intermarriage. If the intermarriage took place six or seven generations previous, genetically today's descendent could be almost totally Native or totally European. In the bush environment there was a much greater opportunity for marrying on the Native side than on the European side, and so most of the blood lines return to Native ancestry. If the offspring married Native in all subsequent generations the sixth generation descendent would then be one-sixty-fourth European, but would still carry the name. The opposite is true of a reversed situation, where each successive marriage involved a European.

The second map (*Fig. 13.2*) illustrates the present division of trapping grounds. This map, when compared with Fig. 13.1, allows a comparison of today's trapping grounds with that of other years. At the time of writing this chapter I did not have all the information related to traplines and the names of the licensed trappers throughout the Kipawa territory. However, my information was complete for the area south of 47° latitude, and it is from this lower, larger half of the territory that I will make the comparison.

Below 47° latitude there were seventeen original family hunting

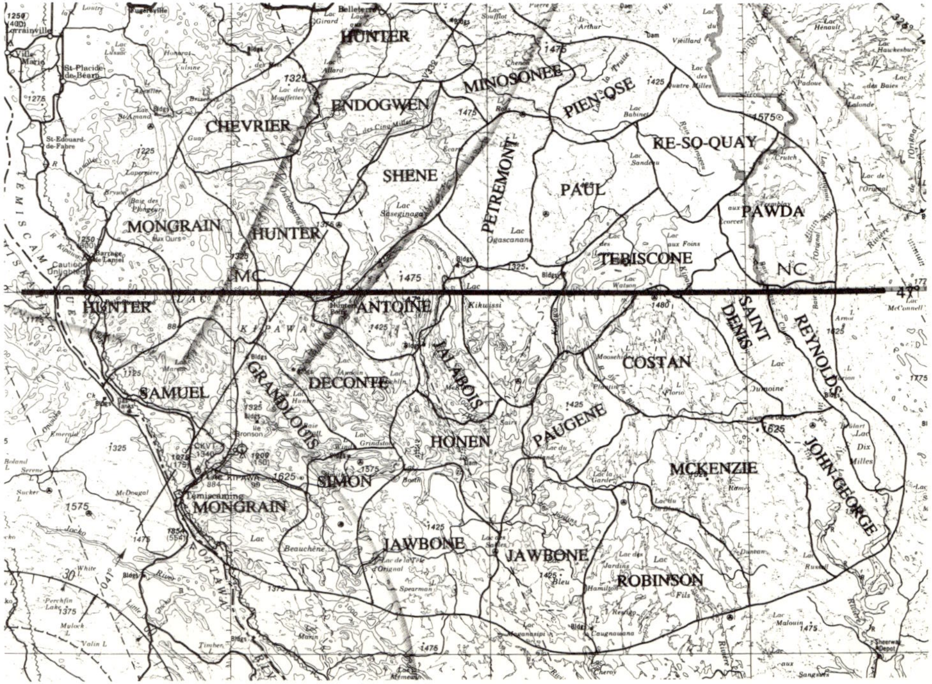

Fig. 13.1. Traditional Hunting Family Territories.

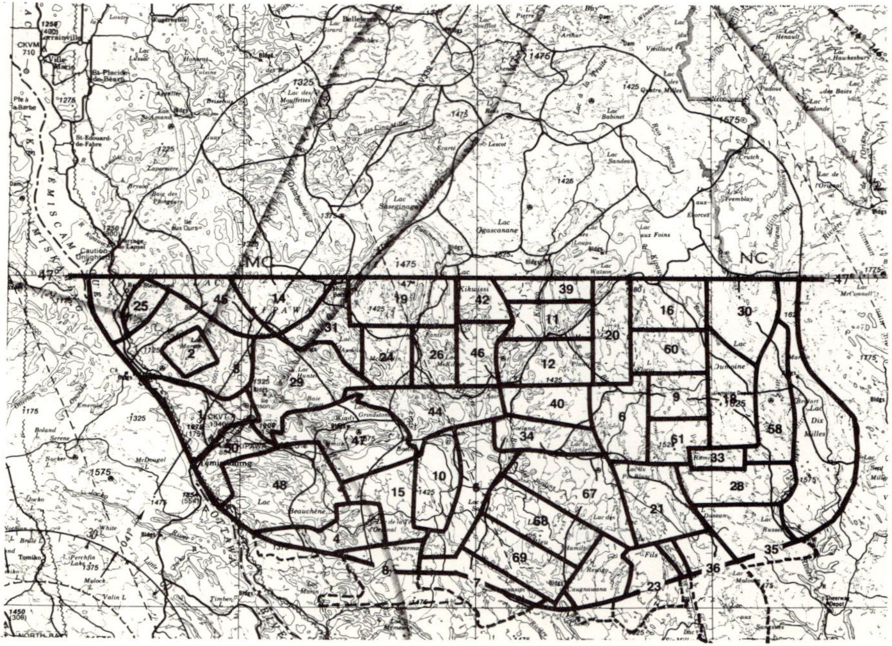

Fig. 13.2. Traplines in Kipawa territory. See Table 13.1 for names corresponding to numbers.

territories, shown on Map 13.1. This figure is reached by taking all the original family territories that are entirely within the greater territory below 47° latitude, together with those territories that straddle the 47° latitude, but that are two-thirds or more on the south side of that latitude. This area which was once occupied by seventeen original hunting families is now divided up into forty-six licensed traplines. Of the forty-six licensed traplines only nine are held by indigenous people or their descendents. A list of names which indicates the licensed trapline holders appears in Table 13.1.

TABLE 13.1   Licensed Trappers in Southern Half of Kipawa Territory

1.	L. Piquette	20.	N. Thibault	42.	G. Gagnon
2.	Vacant	21.	D. Girard	44.	F. McKenzie
3.	C. Fleury	23.	L. Gamelin	45.	P. Bechamp
4.	R. Morin	24.	Vacant	46.	W. Girard
5.	Vacant	25.	A. Dorval	47.	R. Berube
6.	M. Venne	*26.	F. Robinson	*48.	H. Dandy
*8.	R. Chevrier	28.	B. Ledoux	*50.	E. Mongrain
*9.	S. Mongrain	29.	Vacant	48.	J. Ledoux
*10.	J. McDonald	30.	Vacant	60.	A. Gadbois
11.	C. Gagnon	*31.	C. Mongrain Jr.	61.	M. Ledoux
*12.	J. McKenzie	33.	J. Lambert	67.	J. Cyr
*14.	C. Mongrain Sr.	34.	Vacant	68.	P. Morin
15.	A. Bale	35.	L. Belanger	69.	L. Patry
16.	H. Paquette	36.	C. White	71.	L. Dubuc
18.	Vacant	39.	Y. Pelchat		
19.	Vacant	40.	Vacant		

*Indicates Native of Kipawa territory.

It is quite evident from Maps 13.1 and 13.2 that the Native people of Kipawa have been robbed of their heritage. The fundamentals of life are being denied. For a hunting people whose way-of-life has evolved over a period of existence measured in millenia, the abrogation of hunting and fishing rights becomes a form of genocide.

It would be interesting to subject farm lands to the same kind of legislative free-for-all. Suppose that a law governing farm land has been passed that is analogous to the present one governing traplines. Under this law, you tell all the farmers that they do not own their farms any longer. You then divide this county randomly, at the ease and convenience of some bureaucrat, then make a lottery of its distribution. The farmers would find that they have ended up with only one-third of their land areas and quite possibly in a different part of the county. The fact that the homes and other immovable properties must be left behind and that they could quite possibly be moving to unfamiliar farm lands is of no concern to the authorities. Under these conditions the number of farmers who would want to continue farming would rapidly diminish. This is the kind of situation that the Native trapper must contend with only to trap. Then there are those who cannot even get a trapline.

CHAPTER FOURTEEN

Municipal Government

The village of Kipawa is an unorganized community in that it collects no taxes and carries out no public works. Taxes are collected by the Temiscamingue County Council, located at the county seat in Ville Marie. The council is responsible for administering all unorganized communities within the limits of Temiscamingue County. Of late the council has been encouraging the community of Kipawa to organize and form a municipal government. To this point an interim committee has been struck up, composed of a mayor and six counsellors, for the purpose of creating a village council that would carry out the function of municipal government.

A village council that would truly represent the people of Kipawa is impossible under the circumstances that exist in the village at present. One is that the minimum population necessary for forming a municipal government, according to the Quebec Municipal Code, is three hundred residents. The village of Kipawa has a total population of approximately 450. Of these, 230 are Métis, 200 are registered Indians, and the remainder are non-Native. The registered Indians are subject to the Indian Act and as such are governed by a Band council; therefore they cannot be included and the number of eligible residents drops below the legal three hundred. Since it is fairly certain that the village of Kipawa will ultimately become an organized community and that decisions made by the Council will affect all of the people, locally and regionally, it is vitally important that the people of the Band be represented in the council, on a per capita basis.

Second, the interim committee is working towards the amalgamation of Kipawa with Tee Lake and the cottage owners. Tee Lake, a village located three miles south of Kipawa, came into existence as a labor force for Booth Lumber Limited in the 1940's when that company built a lumber mill at the lake of the same name. The cottage owners have their properties along the shorelines of Lake Kipawa and are temporary residents. Both groups are relatively new to the territory.

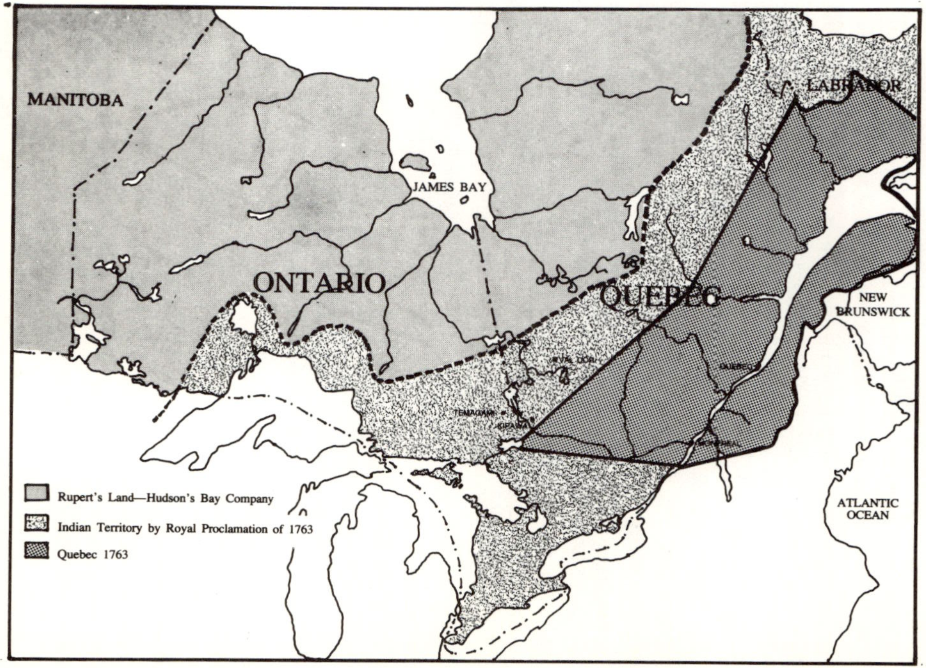

Fig. 14.1. Indian Territory by Royal Proclamation of 1763.

The Native people have identified several fundamental reasons why amalgamation would harm their interests. To begin with, they have not lost sight of the fact that their rights in this territory predate European arrival by countless centuries. The attempt to find common grounds for the development of municipal government with non-Natives would therefore compromise their aboriginal rights. Even though all people in the Kipawa district are friendly toward each other, the Native people have everything to lose and nothing to gain by such an amalgamation. Should it take place, the people of Kipawa would be outnumbered by the cottage owners and Tee Lake residents two to one, and therefore they would be outvoted on all issues where a significant difference in outlook exists between the Native people and the newcomers.

Another important aspect of amalgamation is language. Some of the Native people can speak French, but most cannot, and none has been educated in French. On the other hand the majority of the people who comprise Tee Lake and the cottage dwellers speak that language. Given this, combined with the fact that French is the only official language of Quebec, it means that the business of the council will be conducted in French. The Native people could never be more than ill-informed observers on such a council. Under these conditions there is no possibility of learning the basics of governing as a democratic process. We would once again be submerged with neither voice nor influence to work on our behalf. The choice facing the Native people is whether to tolerate a system that could take their homes and threaten their very existence or to take the necessary steps to form their own village council and learn the business of municipal government by doing it themselves. Learning and achieving the rights of self-government and self-determination (the democratic process) appears to be the only way of lessening the colonial strangulation that continues.

There is another important consideration. When the submission was sent in June 1978 to Quebec for the creation of an organized community, it contained a request to annex a large part of the Kipawa territory to the proposed municipality. If approved, the proposal would in effect legalize the seizure of 565.6 square miles (1,467 square kilometers) of Indian territory. In light of the anti-Native bias of the Ministry of Tourism, Game, and Fish, as reflected by creation and the policing regulations of the Licensed Trapping

Grounds and the *Zone d'Amenagement et de Conservation* systems, little land will be left in which original people of the territory may be allowed to hunt, fish, or even travel.

If amalgamation and annexation were to come about, new developments would occur in the community and on the land affected, but other than being counted like sheep, we would have no role to play. It has happened before; history teaches a vital lesson in this respect. We first welcomed the fur traders and helped them when they needed food, shelter, and furs for their markets. Then things began to change as the fur traders became stronger. The Hudson's Bay Company demanded beaver skins stacked as tall as a muzzle-loader gun as payment for the weapon. This practice of commercial enslavement was common in early times in all areas where the company held a monopoly in the fur trade. The barrel of the old muzzle-loader was anywhere from fifty-one to fifty-five inches, and with the stock the gun would have measured five-and-a-half feet tall. Such a pile of beaver skins in good times represents a whole year's work. Today, such a stack would sell for thousands of dollars. This evil practice was calculated to keep a person in debt to the company till the day he died. As resolutely as the fur companies developed exploitation to an ironclad system, so too did they abandon the people as soon as profits diminished from disease, overtrapping, competition, or whatever reason. When the lumbermen first came to Kipawa they needed the expertise of the Native bushmen in every phase of lumbering. However, when the depression came the Native workers were the first to lose their jobs, an indication of the companies' gratitude and attitude toward the indigenous inhabitants. Land speculation, and by attachment the threat to the homes and lives of the Native inhabitants of Kipawa, is another good example of foreign attitudes and the expressed gratitude of exploitative companies. We must recognize these perils for what they are. To accept a minority position in governing our own community is to take yet another step down that road to self-destruction.

Should the Métis of Kipawa join with Tee Lake and the cottage owners to create a municipality they will alienate themselves from their Native brothers and sisters on the reserve. So closely related are the people that there is not a single Native on the reserve who does not have relatives in the Métis community and vice versa.

Through application of the Indian Act, however, the Department of Indian Affairs makes all final decisions with regard to who is, or is not, an "Indian." Since the law was enacted, Native communities throughout Canada have been divided in this manner.

The question of hunting grounds to the Native people is now a critical one. The traditional family hunting grounds have been swallowed up by clubs and other quasi-jurisdictions that are totally unrelated to the people and the land. Parc de La Vérendrye butts the Kipawa territory at Antiquay Lake on the eastern boundary. The Grand Lake Indian Reserve, which was created in 1928, reaches the middle of the territory at Ogascanan Lake. All the grounds to the west of La Vérendrye Park and the Grand Lake Indian Reserve have been sliced into miniature licensed hunting grounds, and the vast majority have been distributed to outsiders. Then we have the ZEC clubs that could conceivably take in all the open areas for so called sports hunting and fishing. Now we find that the proposed municipality of Kipawa might also be able to control a sizeable area of the territory. This would leave the Native people of Kipawa with only the lots they live on, creating a tiny village in a vast homeland totally controlled by outsiders.

A practical solution to this situation might be for the Native people to set aside the artificial barriers that divide them and form a council that would use both the Indian Act and the Quebec Municipal Code. Are we to become welfare recipients eating baloney and spam while our natural sources of nutritional food become game for so called conservationists and sportsmen? By joining forces the Native people could force discussion on the broad question of land, including such problems as municipalization, ZEC areas, trapping grounds and hunting rights as part of the Aboriginal Rights negotiations.

If the process of municipalization continues on its present course, the day will arrive when Tee Lake and the cottage owners proceed with plans diametrically opposed to the interests of the Native people. Unless we take steps to stop it, only the interests of these outsiders will be served.

Our ownership of the Kipawa territory was acknowledged by Royal Proclamation in 1763. Since that time we have seen those rights ignored, manipulated, and eroded by governments and big business, to a point where our very existence is now at stake. Will municipal government sound the final death knell? The need for new initiatives is urgent. A municipal council combining the reserve with the village of Kipawa could be the first step towards working together on the road to recovery.

Advocates of municipal government allege the following advantages:

(1) such government is a way for people to work together for the common good;

(2) taxes could be collected from the county for local improvements;

(3) the community could apply for provincial and federal assistance in improving the sewage, water, and recreation facilities. Furthermore a village council bringing together both Native groups would take a greater number of initiatives because of the combined strength and unified brain power of the parties concerned.

Other opportunities, as stated by the Province of Quebec in a Policy Paper on Native people, could be exercised on a regional basis from Kipawa. According to the paper:

> The Quebec government would create a *Native socio-economic development fund* for the different regional governments . . . Any socio-economic development program proposed by the Native people and accepted by the Quebec government would be administered by the Native people.

If a plan were devised that would enable the Native people to work together, real progress could be made in the areas of economic, social, and cultural development. It is certain that if we do not establish local government someone else will, and the opportunity of working together will be lost for a long time to come.

CHAPTER FIFTEEN

Land of the Nishnabi—Today and Tomorrow

KIPAWA, QUEBEC
August 30, 1979

Since my last visit to Kipawa, a couple of weeks ago, the village has become a national news item, an item that had come and gone within a space of forty-eight hours. With TV cameras focused on a roadblock the reporter announced that the Native people of Kipawa had blocked the main highway to grab attention for a land claim—a familiar bit of misinformation. It was a protest designed by the people to gain government support in retaining their home lots. (A land claim is always in response to encroachment. It is usually a last resort to save a homeland. Kipawa is a good example of the pressures that may bring about a land claim.) A meeting had taken place between Kipawa's Native people and representatives of the Quebec government. . . .

I returned to my parents' home to help them understand the situation and to hear what Theresa had to say about the events since that first meeting in the church basement. She related the highlights and asked about things that were not clear to her. She began as follows: "The day after that meeting in the church basement, some of the people formed a committee. They felt that they would stand a better chance of fighting Gordon Creek, whoever that is, by working together. They agreed that they'd have to do something different to get government moving, so they talked about a lot of ideas. At last everybody thought that the best thing to do would be to block the road—and that's what we did."

"Did you have any trouble on the blockade?" I asked.

"No, not really, we had a lot of people from all over the north, from Temiscaming and Letang, everywhere. The store owners brought us something to eat and even the businessmen and tourists were on our side. Everybody was friendly, even the cops."

"How did the government know about the blockade?"

"Oh, I forgot to tell you . . . after the committee was formed they got together with some people from the Alliance and wrote up a declaration. It was sent to Quebec, and Ottawa too, I think. Anyway it said that we were going to block the road on the twentieth."

I read the copy of the declaration which was lying on the table. In essence it stated that if either the provincial or federal government did not take action to protect the rights of the Native people of Kipawa by noon, August 20, 1979, the highway to Lake Kipawa would be blocked.

"Did it take long to hear from the government?"

"No, it was pretty fast. The next day I heard that a telegram came from Eric Gourdeau, you know, the guy who works with René Levesque on Native things. He asked for a meeting."

"So that was the meeting you had yesterday?"

"Uh-huh, the meeting was held in the church again. Mr. Gourdeau arrived in the afternoon and the meeting lasted till about seven at night. A lot of people didn't understand what Mr. Gourdeau had to say, but they did get two things straight. First, he promised that no one would be evicted and that he would find out who is claiming our lots—within two weeks. Then he said that in two months time he would be ready to discuss aboriginal rights."

"Did Gourdeau say that the Quebec government would recognize aboriginal rights?"

"I guess that's what he meant. Anyhow he said that the government had recognized aboriginal rights in the James Bay case."

"Did anyone mention the Royal Proclamation?"

"Well I don't know what that's all about, but somebody did say something about some kind of a proclamation and they agreed that Kipawa is in the area. Oh yes, there was also something about a Dorion commission, but I didn't understand what that was supposed to prove either."

"Theresa," I exclaimed. "The Dorion Commission is *extremely* important to our case! That was a commission that met in 1966 on Quebec boundaries. It was that same commission that confirmed this area was designated *Indian Territory* by the Royal Proclamation of 1763."

"And whatever is that supposed to mean?"

"Well, to make a long story short it just means that the Kipawa territory *was not supposed to become part of Quebec without the agreement of the Native people.*"

"And was that ever done?"

"No, never."

"What do you think is going to happen about that?"

"Nothing unless the people get off their rear-ends and do

something about it. This scare about the lots might wake them up. They could take the province to court like the Temagami people have done—with a helluva good chance of winning."

"Gourdeau said something about Native rights being a reality that would have to be respected. He also said that it would make sense for the people and government to talk about compensation. Is he talking about money?"

"Who knows? We won't know unless an injunction is registered by the people."

"Mr. Gourdeau asked a question that stunned a few people. He asked why Native people didn't refuse the dollar-a-year when Booth started charging it forty or fifty years ago?"

"That's a good one all right. And there's more than a simple answer to it. How many ways can you answer that? He might as well have asked why Native people accepted colonialism in the first place."

"Why do you keep bringing up this business of colonialism? It doesn't make sense to me."

"Because there is no other word to describe the situation. The dictionary meaning of colonialism is: 'an alleged policy of exploitation of backward or weak peoples.' So far in Canada it has meant disease, genocide, repression of language, custom and spiritual beliefs, broken promises, land theft, and the plunder of natural resources."

"Do you have to go on like this? I don't like that word colonialism, or immigrant for that matter. Why do you use those words anyway? It doesn't seem right. What's the connection?"

"I don't like to use them either, but we have to deal with the facts. For one thing, you have to remember that there are two kinds of people in Canada—indigenous and immigrant. The indigenous people are the original people of the land, the Natives, ourselves. When I say immigrant, I mean people who have migrated here from around the world in the past four hundred years or so. That word also includes their descendants. Of the immigrant population the Europeans are the most numerous and they control the country. So to be clear about it all, we have to talk about an immigrant government; that is, colonialism."

"It doesn't seem right to call people immigrants if they've been here this long."

"How do you compare 'this long' with always? We were the first here, at least by five thousand years. It's true that some of the immigrants have been here for quite a while, but their attitudes haven't changed. Look at any new problem for indigenous people, and you're faced with the fact that another bunch of immigrants have invaded more of our land. Can't you see the difference? It's the old hat trick. They call it the law, but it really is *colonial* law—or immigrant law, to be more exact. Whatever you call it, that law ignores the rights of indigenous people. That law makes a distinction between the Native and the immigrant; it was called the Indian Act. Laws made by immigrants serve immigrant interests— it's that simple. Where there's a distinction in law, there must be a distinction in terms. That's why we have to use the words immigrant, colonial, and Native.

"Well, there's a lot of people here who don't act like colonialists or immigrants or whatever you call them," she interjected.

"I'm not talking about people so much as I'm talking about *attitudes*," I replied. "I know I'm right about the colonial mentality. You can see the proof everywhere. If I'm wrong, how do you explain this situation in Kipawa? Ask yourself *that* question, and you'll see what I mean."

"The mentality, or whatever you call it—it's hard to imagine."

"It's brainwashing of a sort. Everyone is affected by the colonial mentality: everyone from the woman who marries outside the reserve and loses her Native rights to the Chief Justice of the Supreme Court who *can't do a bloody thing about it*. That brainwashing started from the first day you entered school. At every grade, someone somewhere has tampered with the truth. This tampering is subtle, but it distorts the past and the present. At times the tampering has been both monstrous and blatant. Ever since the Europeans arrived, Canadian history has been full of calculation and bias, and it is from this bias that immigrant attitudes toward the Native have been formed."

"Gosh, I never thought of things that way before! But since we got that letter saying we'd have to pay ten thousand dollars for our own lots, it has made me wonder. I'm still worried about how this will all end. Is this what you mean by colonialism?"

"You're bloody right it is! Colonialism crawls, it never stops. It didn't come to Kipawa overnight or to Canada for that matter. It arrived like a tiny parasite to a healthy body, then it multiplied and spread, all the while sucking blood from the host. Now, after a couple of hundred years, the colonialists cover the whole body and threaten to suck it dry. Colonialism isn't controlled by guns anymore; it's controlled through natural resources, the economy, the land, you name it. It's a greed mentality. It dominates every aspect of society, especially the propaganda machines of the government and the media. It retards real progress in human relations."

"That kind of talk scares me. Do you think that some people actually plan these things?"

"That's for damn sure! Land-grabbing doesn't come about by accident. Never has. The Native people of Kipawa have had one rotten deal after another for years and that has been no accident. It has happened a thousand times across this country and not by accident."

"This business about the land; why can't they just leave Native people alone? Why are they always pushing and pushing for more land; you'd think that they have plenty to live on already? Is this Christian?"

"Land is money . . . and of course for the bosses that's all that matters. But there's something else: Christianity and the ruling classes of Europe used to pretend that they had a divine right over all discovered lands and people. Remember the story of how Jacques Cartier planted his cross in Gaspé Bay back in 1534 and claimed the land in the name of the King of France? Well, that notion hasn't changed a bit. European immigrants still pull that divine right bit."

"OK, since we're going through a rerun of history, how did the newcomers get a foothold in this country, anyway?"

"Well when they first came here, the explorers wouldn't have survived if our Native ancestors hadn't guided, fed, and cared for them. And so who was kind and civilized then? But catastrophe struck and changed history. Our land was disease-free, or so it seems, until the Europeans came; then their diseases devastated our world more than the Black Plague ever did Europe. Each new disease became an epidemic that was repeated, time after time, wherever the European stuck his nose. Up to ninety-five per cent of the population was wiped out. Our race became so close to extinction and the survivors became so weak that instead of resisting the colonialists, they looked to them for salvation. We've been in that fix ever since.

"Gee, that's odd. I've never heard of such a thing. I don't think we were ever told that in school."

Sure, it may seem odd, but it isn't. Good or bad, Native history has always been ignored. The missionaries who wrote about those times sometimes called the epidemics an Act of God—possibly because of their own guilt. They took advantage of the idea to make converts. Later, germ warfare was also used against the survivors.

Theresa thought about that for a moment, then went on to say, "Anyway, to get back to Gourdeau and the meeting, he said that he would be in touch with the committee as soon as he had any information. It does seem as if he really is sincere about what he's doing. The people are furious right now; I'd sure hate to think what would happen if somebody tried to move them."

"Well," I said, "I hope you're right."

KIPAWA, QUEBEC
May 15, 1980

"Theresa, it's more than eight months since that meeting with Gourdeau in August. Have you heard anything about the lots?"

"Not much," Theresa replied. "There have been a few meetings between the Committee and Mr. Gourdeau since last fall. Nothing much seemed to be happening. I did hear this week that the government made a deal with Gordon Creek to buy the land. I think Gourdeau is still looking after it. Anyway, they're saying that we'll have title as soon as the documentation is done."

"Is anybody concerned about the other problems here; I mean about the rest of the land?"

"I think that people are too darned relieved to keep their lots to be jumping into something else. Why? Do you think they should be worried about land?"

"Hell, yes!" I bolted upright in my chair. *"Land is the real issue;* not the lots. You can put your house on a lot, but you sure can't live from it. That land has been our livelihood and our identity. Can't these people see what is happening? If they think they have troubles now, imagine what it will be like for their children if this land-grabbing keeps on."

"To be frank with you I don't follow what you're saying and I'm sure there's a lot of other people who don't understand either."

"Look! For years the people have been forced away from the bush and herded into the village. They should see by now what's been taking place. Number one is the trapping: if the trapline system is allowed to go on, there won't be a single Native in the territory left with a trapline."

"Well, yes, I know there are a few people who are upset because they can't get trapping grounds. What can they do anyway?"

"If only one trapper raises a stink nothing will happen; but if all the Native trappers protest somebody will have to listen. It's pretty much the same for hunting and fishing rights. If ZEC [*Zone d'Amenagement et de Conservation*] keeps on handing the land over to the outsiders, the Native people will find out quickly enough that they can't hunt or fish in what used to be their home territory, or anywhere else for that matter. It's worse than the old clubs; *these* clubs are taking over the whole bloody territory."

"Are you talking about hunting and fishing for sport?"

"I'm talking about hunting and fishing for a *living* as our parents and grandparents used to do. When they get around to parcelling all the land out to clubs, Native people can starve to death or eat spam. I know that sounds grim, but that's exactly what will happen unless Native people get on with the fight for their rights."

"Are you saying there should be a protest on hunting and fishing like you said about trapping, where lots of people would create a real fuss, or whatever?"

"There may be other ways, but unless the people of Kipawa start to work together they'll always be powerless—and that includes you and me. There seems to be only two ways left open. One is to form a municipal council and the other is the land-claim route. The council route means bringing the reserve and the village together to run their own business, instead of letting someone else give the orders. From there they might regain some of their rights in the territory. It would mean trying to work under both the Quebec Municipal Code and the Indian Act at the same time. That'll be a tough job to do and a tough compromise for the Native people to make."

"My gosh, how can you expect people to go for a thing like that? It was bad enough when they started charging taxes on the houses, then they started charging people on the reserve for their cabins in Hunter's Point. Now if we don't do things their way they might close off the bush—ten thousand dollars demanded for our own lots by foreigners—I guess I'm beginning to see what you mean by colonialism and immigrants. It couldn't be worse no matter what the name."

"But then of course labels are not the problem, repression is. Somewhere I read about a wise Mexican once saying that it's better to die on your feet than to live on your knees. It may be time to start considering those ideas. But the time has come to demand our rights to control the resources in Kipawa if we are going to develop our community."

"Well," Theresa declared, "I don't buy that idea about the municipal council. With all the petty politics that go on around here, there's no way the council will work."

"The other way is a land claim done the same way our Nishnabi cousins have filed in Temagami."

"Yes, I know about Temagami. Are you serious? Is it possible we could make a land claim here in Kipawa?"

"Sure. The Temagami Band filed a land caution[25] seven years ago to affirm their entitlement to their homeland. Remember the Royal Proclamation of 1763? I told you about it last summer. The Proclamation covers a good portion of the Nishnabi nation and Indian territory.[26] That was the basis for the claim in Temagami. The Kipawa and Temagami territories join at Lake Temiskaming which, as you know, is the border between Ontario and Quebec."

"What makes you think that something like that would work in Quebec?"

"Well, we won't know until we try, will we?" I replied. "Kipawa territory is covered by exactly the same Proclamation, so the legal basis has to be identical for both provinces. What's important isn't the legal jargon, but the recognition of human and aboriginal rights by the powers that be. The people of Kipawa have a lot of obstacles to overcome before they achieve the objectives we've been talking about."

---

25. As this book goes to press, the Temagami Land Caution is being prepared to go before the Supreme Court of Ontario. The Government of Ontario is suing the indigenous people of Temagami and has asked the court to define Native interest in the land. The caution was filed by the Temagami Band in August, 1973, and is expected eventually to go to the Supreme Court of Canada for a final decision.

26. A map of the proclaimed land appears on Fig. 14.1, p. 156

To My Political Friends

Since May, the battle has continued for the lands in Kipawa. A truth that all governing bodies of this country might do well to remember for the guidance of Canada's future is that the cultural heritage of this country is neither European, Asian, nor African. People of these heritages are, for the most part, firmly established as cultural identities in the countries or continents from which they came. The indigenous peoples are not ethnic peoples, they are nationals in their own lands, and as such are unique to this area of the world. The future reputation and integrity of Canada will be judged by its treatment of the original peoples of this land.

When Native people are forced into courts to protect their homeland and livelihood, no one can deny that it is not only a land claim they are making; it is a counterattack against the invasion of foreigners. As the result of alien claims, Native people have been forced to seek protection under a legal system that is no less alien to them. That is historical fact. The courts of this country would do well to state this fact emphatically, to recognize *Native* law, before rendering judgement on so vital a human concern on the land on which we *live*.

But where do we begin? Most people would agree that history is fundamental to civilized growth. For this reason, indigenous history must be thoroughly researched and the school books rewritten, so that the young people now in school may grow up knowing what really happened in the history of Canada. Diseases imported from abroad played a significant role in the colonization of this country; so did the grab-and-growl ideology of Europeans. If the truth were told, much of the prejudices and misconceptions that mark most Canadian history books would be deleted. History and the fundamental laws of the land are intrinsically entwined. Without truth in both areas justice cannot exist. If this story acknowledges and records the real origins of this country, Canada will have a genuine bench mark for a constitution.

Chief Mike McKenzie and family. From upper left: Loretta, Nancy, Martha, Clarence, his wife Ester, baby Jules, and Mike. In World War II Mike spent three and a half years overseas with the Canadian Army. Upon his return he was abhorred to learn that instead of rewarding the young Natives who had gone to war, their hunting, fishing, and land rights were being systematically taken away. In 1947 he began a move to amalgamate the Brennan Lake, Long Point, and Kipawa Bands. Upon amalgamation he became Chief, a position which he held until 1978. During his term he brought the different groups together and created the Kebaowek Reserve. Mike also served as Vice-President of the Indians of Quebec Association for twelve years.

Mike McKenzie says "After many years of work for my people I have come to realize that most of the problems that are called 'Indian' are not really our problems—they are problems caused by governments. Every problem that we have today was caused by government interference in our land and our livelihood at one time or another. And it goes on.

"I say to governments, treat all people alike. Recognize our heritage and cultural attachment to this land. Allow our people justice, an equal chance to live and grow in our own land. Let us be free, free to work out our own destiny, free to choose our own teachers, free to follow the religion of our ancestors, free to think and act for ourselves, and we will solve our own problems. We are from the soil of this land, and like all things that have grown here, we have a natural power to regenerate. We need only the freedom to do so."